£4
LA2616

KU-136-647

£4
LA2616

PRIME MINISTERS
OF
CANADA

A MARI · USQUE · AD MARE

PRIME MINISTERS
OF
CANADA

Jim Lotz

Bison Books

First published in 1987 by
Bison Books Ltd
176 Old Brompton Road
London SW5
England

Copyright © 1987 Bison Books Ltd

All rights reserved. No part of this publication
may be reproduced, stored in a retrieval system
or transmitted in any form by any means,
electronic, mechanical, photocopying or otherwise,
without first obtaining written permission of
the copyright owner.

ISBN 0 86124 377 3

Printed in Hong Kong

Pages 2-3: *Delegates to the Charlottetown and Quebec conferences, 1864, as painted by Rex Woods from original for Canada's Centennial, 1 July 1967.*

This page: *Sunset over Parliament Hill, Ottawa.*

Contents

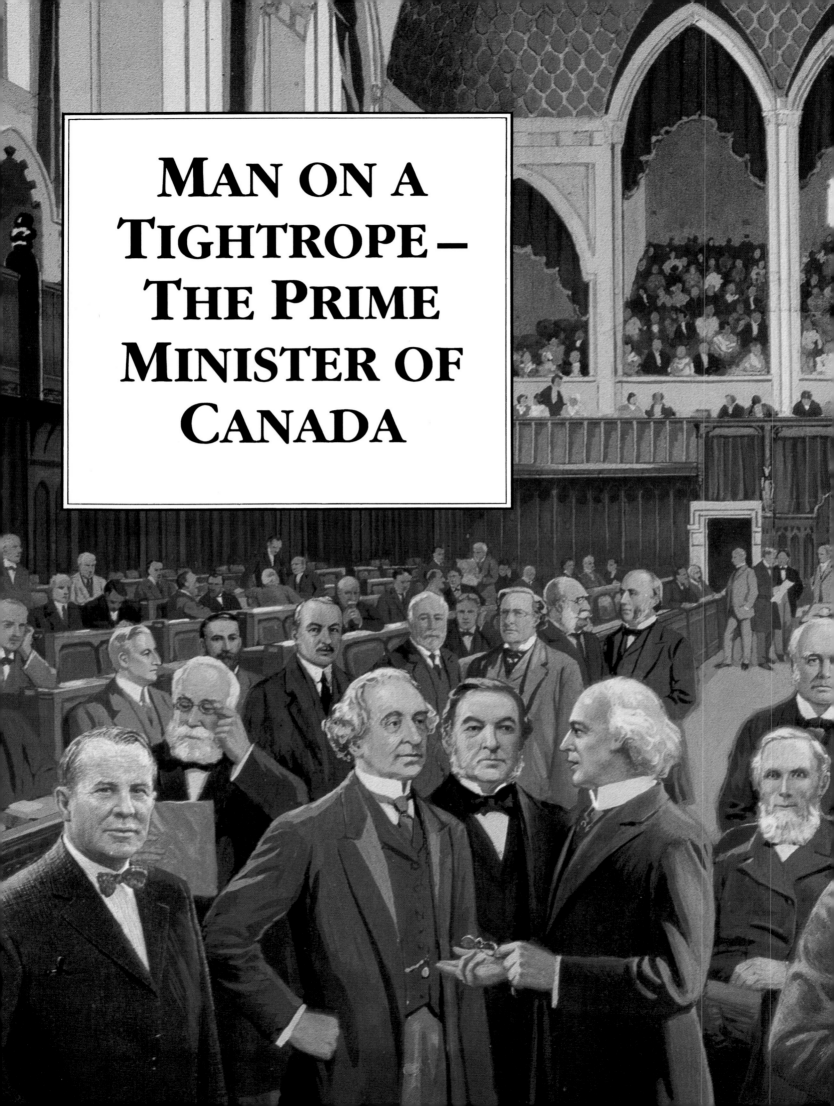

MAN ON A TIGHTROPE – THE PRIME MINISTER OF CANADA

To be Prime Minister of Canada, you need the hide of a rhinoceros, the morals of St Francis, the patience of Job, the wisdom of Solomon, the strength of Hercules, the leadership of Napoleon, the magnetism of a Beatle and the subtlety of Machiavelli.

LESTER PEARSON (1964)

Previous spread: *Canada's Prime Ministers, 1867-1967. In order: Macdonald, Mackenzie, Abbott, Thompson, Bowell, Tupper, Laurier, Borden, Meighen, King, Bennett, St Laurent, Diefenbaker, and Pearson.*

When Benjamin Disraeli became Prime Minister of Britain in 1868, he claimed, 'I have climbed to the top of the greasy pole.' The office of Prime Minister in Britain evolved as the power of the monarch declined. In Britain – and in Canada – Her Majesty the Queen still reigns, but it is the Prime Minister who rules, with the help of his or her Cabinet. The word 'cabinet' means small room, and referred originally to the chamber in which the monarch met with a small group of advisors, the Privy Council, to discuss the running of the country.

During the eighteenth century the kings attended fewer and fewer meetings of their Privy Council as the control of the country began to rest increasingly with Parliament. Parliament controlled the public purse, and the First Lord of the Treasury became the most powerful man in the country. He eventually became known as the 'prime minister.' Sir Robert Walpole, whose Whig party dominated the House of Commons in the first half of the eighteenth century, set the style for the office. As one historian put it, he preferred 'peaceful accommodation to heroic defiance' in all his dealings. The Cabinet met in his house, 10 Downing Street, in London. William Pitt the Younger, who became Prime Minister in 1783, was the first to use the new term to describe his office.

The British had the good sense not to put their constitution in writing. Thus the office of Prime Minister emerged in response to circumstances, and its holders retained a great deal of flexibility. Those who held the office saw their role in running the country in different lights, and reacted in different ways to the problems facing them.

The position and responsibilities of the Canadian Prime Minister are not defined in any official document. As chief minister and head of the executive of the country's parliamentary system, the Prime Minister is normally the leader of the majority party in the House of Commons. He makes appointments, dispenses patronage and has immense power and prestige inside and outside the House of Commons. No matter how well the country is being run or how the economy is faring, if the Prime Minister does not project the right image, he will find himself – and his party – in difficulty. The Prime Minister personifies Canada.

When Sir John A Macdonald became Canada's first Prime Minister in 1867, he had no precedents for the

Great Seal of Canada.

Above: *Privy Council Chamber in Ottawa, where the Cabinet meets.*

Left: *Office of Canada's first Prime Minister, John A Macdonald, who was a leader in bringing about Confederation.*

Since 1918 political parties in Canada have chosen their leaders through membership conventions. All Canadians have been able to hear the proceedings since 1927, when the Progressive Conservative convention was covered by radio, and to see them since 1956, when that party allowed television coverage. Since the media began covering political conventions, they have become a form of theatre. Anyone seeking the leadership of a political party must have a strong power base, large amounts of money and the ability to project his personality on television.

The chosen leader becomes Prime Minister when his party comes to power by winning a majority of seats in the House of Commons. He comes to the office with promises made and debts incurred. The leadership convention probably will have divided the party, which contains individuals with a wide range of views on the best way to run Canada. In governing Canada, the Prime Minister cannot build a Cabinet from the most talented people. He must ensure that all regions, factions, ethnic groups and interests are represented. Alexander Mackenzie, Canada's second Prime Minister, lamented that he had 'no sinecure in trying to keep together a crowd of French Liberals Irish Catholics Methodists Free Traders Protectionists Eastern Province Men Western Men Central Canada men Columbians Manitobans all jealous of each other and striving to obtain some advantage or concession.' No Prime Minister can stay in office unless he has a strong

Above: *Parliament buildings in Ottawa.*

Right: *Queen Elizabeth II and Prince Philip at time of Royal visit 1982.*

Below: *Opening of Parliament in 1982, attended by Queen Elizabeth II upon occasion of signing Canada's new Constitution.*

office. An ocean separated him from Britain, where advice might be sought, but where Queen Victoria persisted in meddling with the running of government. The United States had a government based on the concept of countervailing forces. The founders of that nation, having seen how kings abused their absolute power in Europe, wrote a constitution that ensured that no single agency at the centre of power could dominate government. The Prime Minister of Canada holds a great deal of power in his hands, but his power is not absolute.

power base in Québec and Ontario, where the majority of Canadians live. The people of the West, where many of the country's resources lie, continually complain that their interests are ignored and neglected. Atlantic Canadians have learned the claim that their poverty is due to Confederation and that the region was better off before it joined Canada. Westerners look towards the future and Atlantic Canadians to the past.

When the new Prime Minister of Canada reaches the top of the greasy pole, he finds a tightrope stretching ahead of him. His political fate depends on his ability to walk along this tightrope and to retain his footing as the winds of change buffet him. Not only must he balance national and regional interests, he must also harmonize economic and social demands. Since Canada came into being, certain issues have obsessed Canadians and their leaders – regional disparity, trade, government intervention in the economy, relations with the United States and the defence of a huge land, much

of it sparsely populated.

The problem of protecting the country led to a 'garrison mentality' in which the state stood on guard for Canadians. In recent years Prime Ministers have become painfully aware that foreign policy decisions have an impact on domestic affairs, and that Canada is not an island – or a garrison – complete unto itself. Centripetal forces pull the Prime Minister and his Cabinet into the heart of the country, while centrifugal forces hurl them out to the ends of the earth. Canada has become home to refugees from left and right-wing regimes who have had to rebuild their lives in a new country. Many newcomers came to Canada because of lack of opportunity in their places of birth. Once past the survival stage, they developed a sentimental attachment to their home countries, and in the nineteenth century, many Canadians retained a deep loyalty to 'the old country.' As Canada moved out of the British sphere of influence, it fell under the economic domination of the United States in this century.

Below: *Aerial view of Ottawa showing Convention Centre (large building with spires on left) and Château Laurier (right).*

Since the end of the Second World War, large numbers of immigrants from Europe and Asia have settled in Canada. In handling a great variety of interests lies a Prime Minister's greatest challenge. When Prime Minister Mulroney proposed the idea of free trade with the United States, groups as diverse as artists and union members opposed it. The latter feared the loss of their jobs, the former the disappearance of Canada's cultural identity.

In addition to dealing with the demands of people living in the various regions of Canada, of those from a wide range of ethnic backgrounds and of members of interest groups, the Prime Minister must also keep his constituents happy by spending money in his jurisdiction, or riding. In addition he must protect Canada's interests in the corridors of power in the capitals of the world. In the House of Commons, the Prime Minister must satisfy the demands of the Opposition and keep it off balance, so he must be an effective debater. He must also be skilful in handling small group discussions to ensure that the Cabinet works smoothly. All his actions, and his private life, are scrutinized by the media, intent on reporting conflict and seeking out sin.

If the Prime Minister of Canada's job sounds impossible, then it probably is. Sir John A Macdonald had the phrase 'Canada is a hard country to govern' continually on his lips. Sir Wilfrid Laurier made a similar claim in 1905, as did Lester Pearson in 1965 and Brian Mulroney in 1986. Mackenzie King captured the style of the office in Canada when he claimed that 'The great thing in politics . . . is to avoid mistakes.' He once pointed to a distant church spire beyond a bend in a river. 'If I try to reach that point directly I shall drown,' he said. 'I must follow the curve of the bank and ultimately I shall get there, though at times I may seem to be going somewhere else.'

The personalities of the Prime Ministers of Canada have influenced the role. Government in Canada was informal in the time of Sir John A Macdonald, and he approached the office in a relaxed manner.

Above: Aerial view of Lester B. Pearson Building on Sussex Drive in Ottawa, showing its proximity to Ottawa River. The National Research Council building is seen at left, and the residence of the British High Commissioner (low front surrounded by trees), former home of Canada's first Prime Minister, John A Macdonald.

On one occasion he was carried out of the lunch-room next to the Cabinet chamber drunk, and while negotiating the Treaty of Washington in 1871, he spent 11 weeks in the American capital. William Lyon Mackenzie King sought the advice of the dead on running the country, and ran his Cabinet like the headmaster of a school. Pierre Elliott Trudeau's Cabinet meetings were similar to university seminars. Richard Bennett was autocratic, making all the major decisions himself. John Diefenbaker behaved like a tribal chief, seeking consensus among his Cabinet before acting. Lester Pearson's style resembled that of an affable chairman of the board, while Brian Mulroney seems to see himself as President of Canada Inc. and the country's public relations officer. The Prime Minister of a country like Canada is most effective when he operates like an orchestra leader, bringing out the individual creativity of each player while ensuring that all the instruments are properly tuned and everyone has the same score.

A Prime Minister must have a strong self-image, a sophisticated world view and a style that appeals to his own party and to voters. And he must have luck. Sir Wilfrid Laurier and Pierre Elliot Trudeau came to power – and stayed there – during unparalleled eras of prosperity. Alexander Mackenzie reached the top just as a depression descended on Canada. Some of those who sought the post most avidly, like Richard Bennett and Arthur Meighen, failed to command the hearts and minds of Canadians. Both died disappointed men. Those reluctant to take the office, like Robert Borden and Louis St Laurent, rose to the challenge and provided excellent leadership.

Overall, Canadians have been fortunate in the calibre of their Prime Ministers. Macdonald, Laurier and Mackenzie King, men totally different in style, held the post for 56 years altogether. Much has been made of Macdonald's drinking and of King's interest in spirits of another kind, but these habits did not impair their ability to run Canada to the satisfaction of most Canadians. In the 18 Prime Ministers who have served their country, Canadians can see a reflection of their own hopes, fears, achievements and shortcomings. Looking at the fate of parliamentary democracy in other countries in the Commonwealth, Canadians can consider themselves lucky in the calibre of the men who have held the most powerful political position in the country.

The following short biographies will help readers to appreciate some of the stresses and strains that Canadian Prime Ministers have suffered as they have piloted Canada into being and into a role in the modern world. While some Prime Ministers of Canada have not been particularly attractive individuals, they have all tried to do their best for the country and for Canadians. In this onerous task, they all deserve our respect and compassion.

Left: *Celebration of the 60th anniversary of the Canadian Confederation, in front of Parliament buildings in Ottawa, 1 July 1927.*

OLD TOMORROW

The Rt Hon Sir
JOHN A MACDONALD

1 July 1867 – 5 November 1873
17 October 1878 – 6 June 1891

. . . a rum 'un to look at but a rum 'un to go.

MACDONALD'S DESCRIPTION OF HIMSELF

On 24 July 1886 Sir John A Macdonald gave a speech at Port Moody, the terminus of the Canadian Pacific Railway (CPR). The breeze from the ocean blew the grey hair of the 71-year-old Prime Minister across his forehead. Joseph Pope, his secretary, couldn't help thinking what a triumphal moment it must have been for him.

The CPR linked British Columbia to the new nation. Macdonald had been the prime mover in bringing together Ontario, Québec, Nova Scotia and New Brunswick in 1867, and had become Canada's first Prime Minister on 1 July of that year. On 15 July 1870 the Hudson's Bay Company transferred the Northwest Territories to the new nation. Macdonald created the small province of Manitoba, centred on Winnipeg, in that same year, following Louis Riel's Red River Insurrection resisting the government's attempt to incorporate the Red River colony as a territory without consultation. To lure British Columbia into Confederation, Macdonald promised to build a transcontinental railway, and that province joined Canada on 1 July 1871, but trying to find the money to build the line almost ruined the Prime Minister's political career. On 1 July 1873 Prince Edward Island joined Confederation after Macdonald promised the residents continuous communication with the mainland and the completion of their railway. In 1880, during Macdonald's second ministry, the British government transferred the Arctic Islands to Canada.

Sir John A thus presided over the creation of Canada as a nation. He had come a long way from Glasgow, Scotland, where his birth was registered on 10 January 1815, a few months before the Battle of Waterloo. Macdonald's father, a feckless man with more ambition than ability, failed in business after coming to Canada, in 1820 and became a bank clerk. His thrifty mother provided an anchor as Macdonald grew up in the Kingston area. He later claimed that he had no boyhood, for he left school at 14 and articled with a prominent lawyer at 15. Two years later he was running a branch legal office for his employer, and at 19 started his own practice in Kingston. He served in the militia during the Upper Canada Rebellion of 1837. Then he defended Nils Von Schoultz, a recklessly romantic Polish American who had led the rebels. Macdonald failed to save his client from the gallows, but accepted no fee for his defence.

In 1843, Macdonald, a life-loving man who enjoyed parties and political rallies, married Isabella Clark, with whom he shared a maternal grandmother. After the first year of marriage, Isabella became bedridden and Macdonald immersed himself in politics as she slowly died. He became a steady drinker, like many of his colleagues. A practical man with an astonishing memory for names and faces, Macdonald was no visionary. Elected to the Legislative Assembly of Canada in 1844, he stated: '. . . it is of more consequence to endeavour to develop [Canada's] resources and improve its physical advantages than to waste the time of the Legislature, and the money of the people, in fruitless discussions on abstract and theoretical questions of government.'

Below: *Port Moody, terminus of Canadian Pacific Railway, showing arrival of first train on 4 July 1886.*

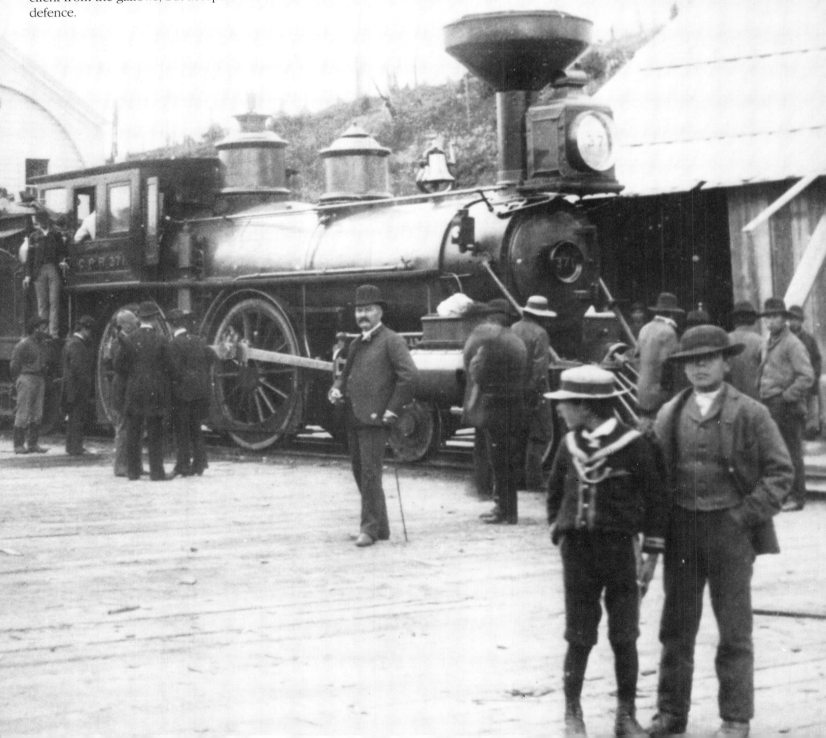

Above: *Delegates from Canada East and Canada West arriving at Charlottetown 1 September 1864 for meeting on Confederation.*

Far right: *Queen Victoria receives John A Macdonald in a private audience in Buckingham Palace 27 February 1867.*

Right: *Delegates from the Canadas, and from Nova Scotia and New Brunswick met in London on Christmas Eve, 1866, to draft the British North American Act leading to Confederation.*

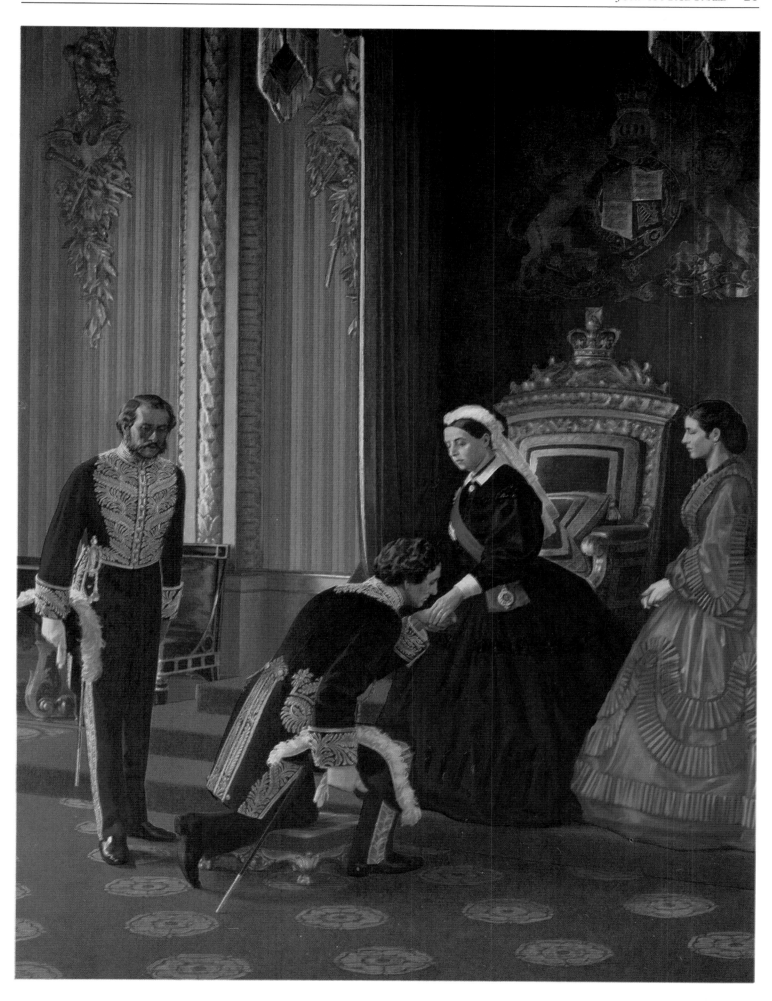

Right: *During construction of railway along the North Shore of Lake Superior workmen inspect their work at Morrison's cut at Jackfish Bay in 1884.*

Below: *Two locomotives with engine and crews pause for a photograph by O B Buell on the newly constructed Nepigon Bridge on the North Shore of Lake Superior.*

NEPIGON BRIDGE

Macdonald's rise to power coincided with the era of the railway, the telegraph and gas lighting. They bound Canadians together and made life more comfortable. In 1860, however, only a fifth of the population lived in cities and towns, where streets turned to mud in winter and the residents choked on dust in the summer. Ottawa did not have piped sewer and water services until 1874, and each year many children died from smallpox, diphtheria, typhoid and measles.

In 1854 Macdonald helped to create the Liberal-Conservative Party, and two years later became joint Premier of the Province of Canada. In pressing for

Above: *Steam shovel at a ballast pit on the North Shore of Lake Superior.*

Above: *On 7 November 1885 the last spike was driven in by Donald Smith, a CPR director, allowing the first transcontinental train, carrying company officers and other notables, to cross over the connection from Ross' rails to Onderdonk's.*

Left: *The track on the North Shore of Lake Superior is so new that the engineers' centre stake is still in position (foreground) and water is tapped in from a temporary chute.*

Right: *House of Parliament with troops sending up a smoke beacon before a crowd assembled in May 1868 for a display of arms.*

Below: SS Rosedale, *first steel steamship to carry cargo from Europe to the heart of North America, is greeted by lakeside crowds upon its arrival in July 1888 at Fort William (now Thunder Bay).*

Above: *Red Ensign used as flag of Canada from 1870 to 1873.*

Confederation, Macdonald favoured a strong, highly centralized federal government. His draft documents stressed the dominance of a central power over provincial bodies. Macdonald jotted down on the margins of his draft of the British North America Act six possibilities for the name of his creation – province, dependency, colony, dominion, vice royalty and kingdom. He favoured kingdom, but called the new nation the Dominion of Canada to avoid upsetting the Americans.

Macdonald, newly knighted, became the Dominion's first Prime Minister in 1867 and Ottawa became its capital. A tall, loose-limbed figure, frail looking, with deep, melancholy eyes and black curly hair, Macdonald dressed flashily and had a penchant for checks. He had a fey side to his nature, once describing himself in a guest book as a 'cabinet maker.' On one occasion he was found drunk in his room, wearing a night shirt and with a rug over him, practicing Hamlet before a mirror.

Macdonald's first wife died in 1857, and he later married Susan Agnes Bernard who wrote: 'Oftentimes he comes in with a very moody brow, tired and oppressed, his voice weak, his step slow; and ten minutes after he is making very clever jokes and laughing like any schoolboy with his hands in his pockets and his head thrown back. . . . I tell him his good heart and amiable temper are the great secrets of his success.' In 1869 their only child, Mary, was born retarded. The Macdonalds tried to involve her in parties and other activities, and Sir John A would read fairy stories to her when he returned from the House of Commons. In 1869 his law partner died, leaving Sir John A responsible for his debts. The Prime Minister's spirit in the face of adversity shone through in a letter to a friend: 'When fortune empties her chamberpot on your head, smile and say "we are going to have a summer shower."' Again and again Macdonald came back from personal tragedy and political defeat with optimism and energy. He knew when to push ahead and when to delay action, and how to make others do his bidding. Macdonald's habit of postponing decisions gained him the nickname 'Old Tomorrow,' but he was also called 'Fox Populi' and the 'Wizard of the North.'

In his first administration, from 1867 to 1873, the Intercolonial Railway between Québec City and Halifax linked central Canada to the Atlantic Ocean. Thinking about the West in 1865, Macdonald noted that he would be quite willing to leave it 'a wilderness for the next half century,' but he feared that 'if Englishmen do not go there, Yankees will.' The Red River Insurrection of 1870, led by Louis Riel, forced Macdonald's government to create the province of Manitoba and to accept separate schools for Catholics and Protestants, and the equality of the English and French languages there.

Left: *Sir John A Macdonald around 1872 when he was in his early fifties, not long after he was knighted.*

When Macdonald promised a railway to British Columbia, he had only the vaguest notions of the difficulties involved in building it. He awarded the contract to a syndicate headed by Sir Hugh Allan, then probably the richest man in Canada. Then Macdonald went on the election trail in 1872. Bribery, corruption and patronage marked politics in Macdonald's time, but the Prime Minister failed to realize that a new nation needed a new morality. To fight the election, Sir John A and his colleagues sought money from Sir Hugh Allan and received $360,000. Macdonald's Conservatives returned to power with a reduced minority and faced an Opposition that claimed that Allan and his backers had bought the right to build the Canadian Pacific Railway with bribes. In 1873 the Liberal press broke open the Pacific Scandal by publishing the most famous telegram in Canadian history, which was from Sir John A to Sir John Abbott, legal advisor to the CPR. It read: 'I must have another ten thousand; will be the last time of calling; do not fail me; answer today.'

In vain did the Prime Minister claim that 'not one single farthing that has passed through my hands was expended improperly or contrary to the laws.' In vain did the government set up a royal commission to investigate the matter. Then, as now, the Prime Minister had to be like Caesar's wife – he had to be above suspicion even if he had done no wrong. A cartoon by J W Bengough showed Macdonald saying 'I admit I took the money and bribed electors with it. Is there anything wrong with *that?*' Beneath Macdonald's feet ran a quotation from *The Mail* of 26 September 1873: 'We in Canada seem to have lost all idea of justice, honour and integrity.' With the party in disarray, the Opposition howling and the electorate dismayed, Macdonald's government resigned and was defeated in the next election. Plain Sandy Mackenzie, an honest man above reproach, became Prime Minister just as the country plunged into a depression.

Sir John A returned to office in triumph in 1878. He introduced high tariffs, particularly on imports from the United States, which strengthened the grip of central Canadian manufacturers on the economy. When he awarded the contract to build the Canadian Pacific Railway to a group headed by George Stephen, he also provided a subsidy of $25 million plus 25 million acres of land. The huge cost of running the rails across Canada almost bankrupted the syndicate.

A crisis in the West saved the railroad and Macdonald. The Indians of the Plains had once been self-sufficient, deriving all they needed – and their identity – from the buffalo. When white hunters slaughtered thousands of these beasts, the Indians, wards of a distant and uncaring government, drifted into poverty and despair. The Métis (people of mixed white and Indian blood) also saw their way of life threatened as surveyors, settlers and new regulations hemmed them in, but Macdonald refused to listen to their complaints. Louis Riel returned from

Left: Macdonald introduced a policy of high tariffs, especially on imports from the US, and brought profits thereby to manufacturers and a slice of the pie to workers and farmers.

exile in the United States at the request of Métis leaders, who demanded to be self-governing, and led the Saskatchewan Rebellion in 1885. After some initial successes the rebels faced an army under a British general who had transported his troops out west on the Canadian Pacific Railway. The Métis were defeated at Batoche in May 1885 and lost their struggle to maintain their free life. However, the builders of the CPR received the government funds

Below: Soldiers make themselves comfortable as they head across the plains to quell the Saskatchewan Rebellion in 1885.

Above: *Both parties opposed Riel's election to Parliament.*

Above: *Louis Riel, a Métis who headed the late 19th-century rebellion in the western provinces, symbolized the bitter French-English divisions that still plague Canada. Hanged for treason, he remains a "hero" of national stature.*

they needed to complete the line because of their part in putting down the Riel Rebellion.

Tried for treason in Regina, Louis Riel died with dignity on the gallows on 16 November 1885. The Cabinet and Queen Victoria rejected pleas for clemency. Macdonald's famous claim before Riel's execution – 'He shall hang though every dog in Québec bark in his favour' – echoes down the corridors of Canadian history as an indicator of the lack of concern by Conservatives for French Canadian sensitivities or for alternative visions of Canada.

On Macdonald's first and only trip to the West in 1886, he met Chief Crowfoot near Calgary. The Indian complained of the damage done by sparks from the 'fire wagons' that set fire to the prairie. Macdonald pointed out that the railroad was doing much good and that the Indians should help themselves, 'like white men,' by growing good crops.

At a Toronto gathering in 1884 to celebrate his 40 years in Parliament, Sir John A had described himself as 'a feeble old man.' A voice from the audience shouted, 'You'll never die, John A.' Like many another powerful politician, Macdonald preferred followers around him rather than rivals or potential leaders. In their campaign in 1891 the Conservatives used the slogan, 'The Old Man, the Old Flag, and the Old Policy.' Macdonald made an issue of the Liberals' plans for free trade with the United States, claiming it was a prelude to annexation. He asked Canadians to proclaim themselves 'among the most dutiful and loyal subjects of our own beloved Queen.'

Macdonald had a highly ambivalent attitude towards Britain, however. He had established the post of Canadian High Commission to Britain in 1880, and strove to establish a partnership with the mother country. The colonial connection might be a chain, but to him it was 'a golden chain' and he was 'glad to wear the fetters.' At the same time, he declared that there was no place in the government of Canada for 'overwashed Englishmen, utterly ignorant of the country and full of crotchets as all Englishmen are.' Nevertheless, at election time Macdonald wrapped himself in the Union Jack on the hustings declaring, 'A British subject I was born – a British subject I will die.' On 5 March 1891, the Conservatives resumed power.

Always a hard worker, Macdonald often stayed late in the House of Commons and then attended to official business after midnight. In May 1891 he suffered a slight stroke, but maintained his usual routine. On 23 May, Macdonald returned home tired from a Cabinet meeting and played host at one of the couple's regular Saturday evening dinner parties. Four days later he had another stroke. The tough old Scot, then 76, recovered, but on 29 May came the final stroke. A message went to the House of Commons that his condition was 'quite hopeless.' At 10.15 on the evening of 6 June 1891 Canada's first Prime Minister died peacefully and without pain. His second wife died in 1920 and their daughter Mary in 1933.

Plain Sandy

The Rt Hon
Alexander Mackenzie

7 November 1873 — 9 October 1878

*Consequences had to go to pieces
before Alexander Mackenzie.
God give us more such as he,
honest and true.*

S H BLAKE after the funeral of Mackenzie (April 1892)

Right: *Alexander Mackenzie, a
'Reformer' among the Liberals
and their first Prime Minister.
Because of his Scottish
background perhaps, he was
often called 'Plain Sandy.'*

A Tory banner in the election of 1878 claimed that 'Sandy's no sic a man as our Sir John.' That phrase sums up the strengths and the weaknesses of Alexander Mackenzie, Canada's second Prime Minister. The election of his Liberal government in 1873 shows two themes that are consistent in Canadian politics. The first is that voters tend to throw out governments they don't like rather than voting in those that they believe will be able to handle the country's problems. The second is that they tend to support parties whose Prime Ministers have very different characteristics from their predecessors. Mackenzie, red bearded, with bright eyes and a straight mouth, a teetotaller and a man of integrity, had no skills in managing men and lacked Macdonald's guile and charm. He inevitably went for principle over expediency when faced with a decision. Canadians called him 'Plain Sandy,' and he described himself as 'Clear Grit – pure sand without a particle of dirt in it.'

Born in a crofter's cottage near Dunkeld, Scotland, in January 1822, Mackenzie followed his heart to Canada 20 years later when his sweetheart, Helen Neil, moved with her family to a farm near Kingston in Ontario. A stone cutter by trade, Mackenzie prospered and went into business as a contractor with his brother. He married Helen in 1845, but she died seven years later, and only one of the couple's three children survived infancy. Mackenzie later married Jane Sym, who also came from his home county of Perthshire.

Settling in Sarnia, Ontario, Mackenzie became a 'Reformer' as pre-Confederation Liberals were called. In the early 1850s he edited the *Lambton Register*, a reform newspaper. Elected to the Legislative Assembly of Canada in 1861, Mackenzie became an able debater and a good organizer. He won a seat in the first Canadian House of Commons in 1867, and also served in the Ontario legislature. But after only two years in the new Parliament, Mackenzie wished he were 'clear of this abominable life.' Nevertheless, the Liberals chose him as their leader in 1872, and like many other Prime Ministers, Mackenzie took up the post reluctantly when Macdonald's government fell in 1873.

Plain Sandy took office just as a depression settled on Canada, and government revenues fell. To balance the national budget, he raised tariffs at a time when Liberals equated them with original sin and saw free trade as the way to economic salvation. Mackenzie served as Minister of Public Works and pushed ahead with the transcontinental railway, but he had only the vaguest notions of the difficulties involved in completing it. He put his finger on a map of British Columbia one day, found it rested on Vancouver Island, and declared, 'Let that be the terminus of the Pacific Railway.' He tried to make the railway self-supporting by linking the waterways in the West with stretches of track. This approach failed to satisfy Canadians fired by Macdonald's vision of steel rails traversing the empty West, and it certainly did not please the people of British Columbia at all. Mackenzie also neglected to recruit a strong right-hand man to protect his party's interests in Québec. Indeed, he had little talent in his Cabinet.

Above: *Mackenzie's notions about the difficulties of constructing a transcontinental railway tended to be vague and his discussion of it didactic.*

Left: *Work at the St Gabriel Locks during the enlargement of the Lachine Canal, 1821-25, connecting Lake St Louis with the St Lawrence River at Montreal.*

Right: *Alexander Bell triumphantly completes first long distance call from Paris, Ontario, to Brantford, 10 miles away, on 10 August 1876.*

Below: *During the Cariboo Gold Rush the Royal Engineers pushed a 400-mile road through the Fraser Canyon to reach the gold fields of the northern interior.*

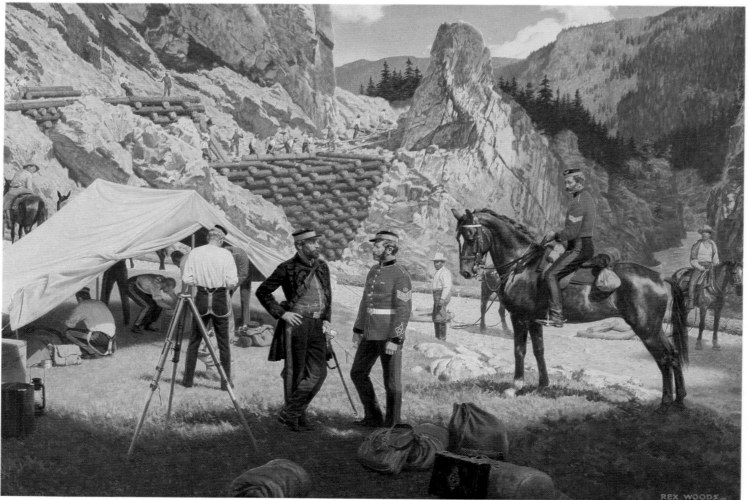

Mackenzie sought to free Canada from British domination. He refused a knighthood, and told Disraeli that 'we are all but ruined from first to last by English diplomacy and treaty making and we would have no more of it at any price.' Mackenzie's style came across in his claim that 'loyalty to the Queen does not require a man to bow down to her man-servant, or her maidservant – or her ass.'

In better times and in another era, Mackenzie's latent greatness and honesty might have made him a memorable Prime Minister. A lonely man, the Prime Minister claimed that he was ambitious only 'to succeed in governing the country well and without reproach.' He sought to run Canada the way he built his houses – straight and true. Mackenzie wore himself out in office. By 1878, as the Governor-General Lord Dufferin put it, the Prime Minister resembled 'a washed-out rag and limp enough to hang upon a clothesline.' During his tenure the Liberal government succeeded in establishing the Supreme Court of Canada and the Royal Military College of Kingston. It also passed legislation to ensure cleaner elections, and the one in September 1878 was the first election ever to feature the secret ballot.

Sir John A Macdonald had put together his National Policy to cure the national depression and worked his magic in the hustings of that election. He proposed raising tariffs, but did not stress that aspect of his policy in his presentations. Although Macdonald lost his seat in the 1878 election, the voters swept Old Tomorrow's Conservatives back into power.

Plain Sandy hung on to the Liberal leadership until 1880, and then kept his seat in the House of Commons until he died in April 1892, less than a year after Macdonald. At the end, he whispered: 'Oh, take me home.'

In later years Canadians may well have longed for the leadership of a man of Mackenzie's calibre as they witnessed the efforts of Macdonald's successors in running the country.

Above: *Lord Dufferin, Governor-General of Canada from 1872 to 1878, viewed Mackenzie disparagingly.*

Left: *Despite Lord Dufferin's poor esteem, Prime Minister Mackenzie achieved such lasting institutions as the establishment of the Supreme Court of Canada, the Royal Military College of Kingston, and, in 1878, the first secret ballot.*

MACDONALD'S SUCCESSORS

The Rt Hon Sir

JOHN J C ABBOTT

16 June 1891

– 24 November 1892

The Rt Hon Sir

CHARLES TUPPER

1 May 1896 – 8 July 1896

The Rt Hon Sir

MACKENZIE
BOWELL

*21 December 1894
– 27 April 1896*

The Rt Hon Sir

JOHN SPARROW
THOMPSON

*5 December 1892
– 12 December 1894*

> *Sir John had so much tact as well as strength that he managed to keep the incongruous racial and religious sections in his Cabinet working together but now all are working against one another. . . .*

LADY ABERDEEN on Sir John Thompson (March 1895)

A visitor to Parliament, watching Sir John A Macdonald in action, said, 'If anything were to happen to him, the Conservative Party would not hold together for ten days.' A Conservative friend corrected him, saying 'Not for ten minutes.' Over the years the Conservative party in Canada has developed a reputation for destroying its own leaders and for backbiting and infighting. These characteristics appeared among Macdonald's immediate successors, and the first Prime Minister's true greatness can be appreciated in the light of the chaos into which his government descended as four others tried to fill his shoes.

In 1890 the Manitoba legislature decided to abolish the state-supported Catholic school system. The Manitoba School Question heightened tensions between Catholics and Protestants, Métis and settlers, Ottawa and Manitoba. Instead of putting in a strong man who could have acted swiftly and fairly, the Conservatives selected Senator Sir John Abbott to succeed Sir John A Macdonald, and he became Prime Minister in June 1891. A burnt-out corporation lawyer, Abbott claimed that he had been made Prime Minister 'because I am not particularly obnoxious to anyone.' He also said that he hated 'notoriety, public meetings, public speeches, caucuses, and everything of which is apparently the necessary incident of politics.' Acting simply as a caretaker, he handed over the government to Sir John Thompson in November 1892.

Thompson, a Halifax lawyer and the son of an Irish immigrant, had converted from Methodism to Catholicism. He served briefly as Premier of Nova Scotia, then became a judge of the provincial Supreme Court at the age of 36 in 1882. Portly, clean shaven and happily married with five children, Thompson had little taste for politics. A Tory colleague claimed that Thompson would not 'consider whether a thing is good for the party until he is sure it is good for the country.' Searching for fresh talent to bring life to his tired government, Sir John A Macdonald offered Thompson a place in his Cabinet, and he became Minister of Justice and Attorney-General on 26 September 1885. Prime Minister Macdonald claimed that finding Thompson was 'the great discovery of my life,' although he was 'a little too fond of satire and a little too much of a Nova Scotian.' Thompson did not defer to Macdonald, and became a close and trusted friend.

Lady Aberdeen, wife of the Governor-General, noted approvingly that as Prime Minister, Sir John Thompson soon became adept at handling his Cabinet. However, he had little time in office to display his talents. On 12 December 1894 Sir John Thompson was made a member of Queen Victoria's Privy Council. The only other Canadian so honoured had been Sir John A. The ceremony lasted only 20 minutes, and then the company adjourned for lunch. Clad in morning dress, with black knee breeches and silk stockings, Thompson sat down to eat. Then he fainted. On recovering in another room, he remarked that 'it seems too weak and foolish to faint like this.' Sitting down next to the Queen's doctor, the Prime Minister complained of a pain in his chest. Then he slumped over – dead.

With Thompson died any hopes that the Conservatives had of staying in power. The Conservatives selected Sir Mackenzie Bowell to replace him. Born in England, Bowell had started his working life as a printer's devil, becoming editor and publisher of the *Intelligencer* in Belleville, Ontario. He also became Grand Master of the Orange Order of Protestants. Elected to Parliament in 1867, this 'tiny, stupid man' who looked like 'a bitter Santa Claus,' in the words of one writer, hated Catholics and Grits. He upset the Manitoba government and most of his Cabinet

colleagues with the way he handled the Manitoba School Question. Seven resigned, and Bowell called them a 'nest of traitors.'

Sir Joseph Pope, clerk to the Cabinet, wrote feelingly of the chaos into which government drifted under Bowell:

> . . . *days of weak and incompetent administration by a Cabinet presided over by a man whose sudden and unlooked-for elevation had visibly turned his head . . . a ministry without unity or cohesion of any kind, a prey to internal dissensions until they became a spectacle to the world, to angels and to men.*

Bowell sought to replace his lost Cabinet members, but every prominent Conservative boycotted him. Into the power vacuum left by Bowell's incompetence galloped Sir Charles Tupper, a most remarkable man.

Born in Amherst, Nova Scotia, in July 1821, Tupper studied medicine at Edinburgh University. He graduated in 1843 and practised medicine in between his political activities. In the provincial election of 1855 Tupper took Joseph Howe's seat in Cumberland County, became Premier of Nova Scotia in 1864 and championed Confederation. A broad-shouldered man lacking a sense of humour, Tupper's reputation with women gained him the nickname 'The Ram of Cumberland.' He entered Macdonald's Cabinet in 1870, and as one wit put it, 'Sir John A Macdonald steered the ship of state, while Tupper provided the wind.' In appearance and temperament, the short, stout, caustic Tupper complemented the tall, thin, witty Sir John A. According to a fellow MP, Tupper looked 'as if he had a blizzard secreted somewhere about his person.'

Tupper held the post of Minister of Railways while also serving as Canadian High Commissioner in Britain after 1880, at a salary of $10,000 a year. In 1885 he received $100,000 in Canadian Pacific Railway stock as a gift from the syndicate that built the line. While in Canada in 1896, Tupper took over from Bowell as Prime Minister. Sworn into office on 1 May 1896, Tupper lasted 69 days as Prime Minister – a Canadian record. Losing his seat in the election of 1900, Tupper retired to Vancouver, then moved to England and died there in 1915 at the age of 94. His obituary in the London *Times* praised his 'driving power,' but it also noted that Tupper lacked a vital quality as Prime Minister – he had 'something like contempt for compromise.' In contrast his Liberal successor as Prime Minister, Sir Wilfrid Laurier, came to be known to Canadians as 'The Great Conciliator.'

Above: *Fortune seekers from all parts of Canada streamed to the Klondike in the Yukon in the 1890s to hunt for gold. This group of miners are at a staked-out claim called No 1 Eldorado Creek.*

Left: *Gold miners trudged over rock, snow and ice into the Canadian Arctic, effectively bringing about the first real opening of the North.*

THE GREAT CONCILIATOR

The Rt Hon Sir

WILFRID LAURIER

11 July 1896 – 6 October 1911

. . . A man who had affinities with Machiavelli as well as with Sir Galahad.

J W DAFOE, *Laurier* (1922)

Right: *Sir Wilfrid Laurier, first French Canadian Prime Minister, in 1869, at the age of twenty-eight. Six feet tall, charming, he was an effective orator and debater.*

On 4 May 1864 the valedictorian of the Undergraduate Law Society of McGill University pledged that he would give his whole life to 'the cause of conciliation, harmony, and concord among the different elements of this country of ours.' In these words, Henri Charles Wilfrid Laurier, who became Canada's seventh Prime Minister 32 years later, set out his goals. Born in St Lin, Québec, in 1841, Laurier grew up in humble circumstances. His mother died when he was five, and his father, Carolus, a land surveyor, remarried. Wilfrid had a happy childhood. The father, ambitious for his son, sent him to nearby New Glasgow. In this Scottish settlement young Laurier learned English and received a sound basic education. Then Laurier attended La Collège de l'Assomption 20 miles from home, where he received the traditional education of a bright Québec boy. The study of Greek and Latin, combined with prayer and strict discipline, prepared the best and the brightest of the province's youth for the priesthood.

Instead of becoming a priest, Laurier moved to Montreal to article with a Liberal lawyer and took courses at McGill University, which had been set up as a secular institution to counter the influences of the Catholic classical colleges. Laurier matured within the widening gap that existed between the traditional society of Québec, which focused on the family and the farm, and the bustling world of business in the cities and factories of an industrializing province. At college Laurier learned public speaking, one of the basic political skills, and became an effective orator and debater. Concerned about his health, Laurier moved to Arthabaska, near Victoriaville, in Québec's Eastern Townships. Here he edited a small Liberal newspaper until clerical condemnation of its contents forced it to close. Made aware early of the power of the church, Laurier then practised law. In 1868 he married Zoë Lafontaine, and five years later won a seat in the provincial election.

When Alexander Mackenzie's Liberals came to power in 1873, Laurier went to Ottawa as an MP. He gave his maiden speech in French, but spent much of his time in the Parliamentary Library. Joining the Cabinet in 1877, he soon concluded that 'our party is going to the dogs.' One Grit complained that Laurier would never make a leader – 'he has not enough of the devil in him.' At a meeting in Montreal in 1885 to protest the hanging of Louis Riel, Laurier declared that if he had been born on the banks of the Saskatchewan he would have 'shouldered a musket to fight against the neglect of government and the shameless greed of speculators.' Once called 'Lazy Laurier' by the newspapers, the man from St Lin became party leader in 1887. Over six feet tall and elegantly clad, Laurier charmed everyone he met. He began to rebuild the Liberal party and to develop a national structure for it. In 1893 he organized a convention in Ottawa to work out a new programme, and three years later led his party to victory when the Conservatives ran out of steam.

Laurier, the first French Canadian Prime Minister, came to power as the British Empire reached its zenith. The enthusiasm and optimism that marked the end of the century gave way to the comfortable world of the Edwardians. Here all seemed for the best in the best of all possible worlds – if you belonged to the prospering middle and upper

population rose from just under five million in 1891 to over seven million in 1911, creating a great demand for new goods and services. Like many other political visions though, this one soon became a nightmare. The two new railway lines across the country proved very expensive, and could not pay their operating costs, thus adding to the national debt.

In 1905 Manitoba expanded its boundaries, and Saskatchewan and Alberta came into being. Laurier did not permit the establishment of separate schools in the new provinces, and he skilfully defused the Manitoba School Question through compromise, lobbying at the Vatican and using gentle persuasion – the hallmarks of his style. Instead of separate schools, Catholics in Manitoba received permission to provide some religious education for their children in the existing ones.

Laurier attracted strong and capable men to his Cabinet, claiming in 1905 that 'as the nineteenth century had been the century of the United States, so the twentieth century would be the century of Canada.' During the first decade of the century, Canadian businessmen formed large organizations to produce and market steel, bread, paint and cement. They also invested their money in transportation systems and power plants in South America. On the Prairies, farmers banded together to establish co-operatives and to buy their own grain elevators.

The Prime Minister saw the government as an umpire between labour and management, not as an active intervenor. He set up a Department of Labour in 1900 and the government passed a number of acts aimed at reconciling workers and bosses, but the Liberals did not explore the causes of the rising discontent in industry. In 1901 Marconi sent the first

classes. As the Prime Minister's chestnut hair turned grey, it looked as if he were wearing a halo. With his 'silver tongue,' Laurier promoted his 'sunny ways' in an era of rising expectations.

Canada boomed during the Laurier years. The wheat from the West went to feed the expanding cities in Europe. From them came a stream of immigrants eager to start a new life in a new land. In 1903 Laurier had a vision of railways opening up the northern parts of the Prairies, stimulating wheat production and an influx of immigrants. Canada's

Above: *Laurier came to power in an era of enthusiasm and optimism.*

Left: *In 1897 Laurier worked out a compromise on the question of English and French schools.*

transatlantic 'wireless' message from Signal Hill in Newfoundland. Eight years later the *Silver Dart* left the ice at Baddeck in Cape Breton, marking the first manned power flight by a British subject in the Empire. These achievements fed the sense of euphoria that pervaded Edwardian Canada where progress was equated with material improvement. No one could foretell how these new devices would be used.

As the economy hummed along, Laurier sought to act as a mediator as Canada's relationships with Britain and the United States changed. In 1897 he travelled with Zoë to England to attend the Diamond Jubilee of Queen Victoria, and he received red-carpet treatment. Laurier gave numerous speeches, reviewed the British fleet, received honorary degrees from Oxford and Cambridge, stayed at Windsor Castle and Buckingham Palace and received his knighthood from the Queen herself.

After the soft soap came the hard sell. Joseph Chamberlain, Britain's Colonial Secretary, solicited help from Canada to stimulate trade, fight the South

Above: *Laurier received red-carpet treatment and was knighted when he attended the Queen's Diamond Jubilee in 1897.*

Left: *House of Commons in session in 1897 soon after Laurier became Prime Minister.*

Right: *Parade up Jaspar Avenue in Edmonton on 1 September 1905 when Alberta became a province.*

Left: *Voters outside 'Polling Station' in Saskatchewan on 3 November 1904 to decide issue of joining the Dominion of Canada as a province. The results were affirmative, and provincial status made official in 1905.*

Below: *The O'Reilly wagon train en route from Vermilion in Alberta to Wainwright, Alaska, in the Spring of 1906.*

Above: *Lady Zoë Laurier (née Lafontaine).*

Right: *Queen Victoria and escort on 22 June 1897 during celebration in London of the Diamond Jubilee.*

African war and counter Germany's growing naval might. In response Canada granted Britain preferential tariffs. This led Rudyard Kipling to write a poem entitled 'Our Lady of the Snows,' in which Canada describes itself as 'Daughter . . . in my mother's house, but mistress in my own.' This comforting, cosy image proved illusory when Laurier compromised about sending Canadian troops to South Africa to fight the Boers. English Canadians favoured the idea, but French Canadians felt they had much in common with those fighting an alien invader. So the Canadian government shipped a thousand volunteers to South Africa, where they became the financial and political responsibility of Britain.

In his dealings with the United States, Laurier had to contend with a country powered by expansionism and jingoism under President Teddy Roosevelt. In 1898-99 Laurier failed to settle the Alaska-Canada boundary by direct negotiation, and the matter was referred to an international tribunal made up of three Americans, two Canadians and the British Lord Chief Justice. The Englishman favoured the American claim, which cut off northern British Columbia and the Yukon from the sea. When the Americans won Laurier described them as 'very grasping in their national actions, and determined on every occasion to get the best in any agreement they make.'

COPYRIGHT

But the only sure shield against American imperialism was Britain's fleet. Canada had no navy and only a handful of soldiers to guard its long borders. Britain wanted Canada to provide money for the British dreadnoughts as the German fleet expanded, but Laurier decided to give Canada its own navy, and introduced a bill on 12 January 1910 to do so. If war came, the Canadian fleet would be under Imperial control, if Parliament approved.

Laurier rode through his years of power like a white knight, oblivious to the mud beneath his horse's hooves. As described in the *Encyclopaedia Britannica* of 1910, the Prime Minister was 'an individualist rather than a collectivist' who opposed 'the extension of the state into the sphere of private enterprise.' In Winnipeg, J S Woodsworth, a Methodist minister who worked among the poor in the North End, exposed the despair and misery there in *Strangers Within Our Gates* in 1909 and *My Neighbors* in 1911, revealing that many immigrants had not made a new life for themselves in Canada but were being brutally exploited. Domestic problems like this, however, did not lead to Laurier's downfall; fears of an American takeover did.

Relations with the United States improved after President William Taft took office in 1909. He sought a tariff agreement with Canada, and Laurier prepared a reciprocity agreement with the United States. The Conservatives played on the fear of many Canadians that the United States wanted to annex Canada, and one of their campaign posters showed

Far left, top: *The first stores in the town of Dawson in the Yukon.*

Far left, bottom: *Scales and summit of Chilkoot Pass, Alaska, around 1898.*

Above: *Joseph Chamberlain, Britain's Colonial Secretary, 1895-1903, who pursued a vigorous policy to promote trade with Canada.*

Right: *Sir Wilfrid Laurier (seated) with W L Mackenzie King in 1915.*

Laurier begging on his knees in front of Uncle Sam. Farmers in the Canadian West favoured free trade, for they would then be able to buy manufactured goods from south of the border instead of from eastern Canadian manufacturers.

During the election of 1911, Laurier set out the frustrations that beset him as he tried to follow the middle path in politics:

I am branded in Québec as a traitor of the French, and in Ontario as a traitor to the English. In Québec I am branded as a Jingo, and in Ontario as a Separatist. In Québec I am attacked as an Imperialist, and in Ontario as an anti-Imperialist. I am neither. I am a Canadian.

He was genuinely shocked when the voters rejected him and Sir Robert Borden's Conservatives came to power in 1911. When war broke out in 1914, Laurier supported Canada's involvement, but did not favour conscription. In 1917 Borden formed a Unionist government to bring Canadians together in the war effort. Many Liberals deserted Laurier to join it, and Borden offered him a place in it. The former Prime Minister refused, and around him gathered the remnants of the once powerful ruling party. Among them was William Lyon Mackenzie King, a future Prime Minister who also opposed conscription. A photograph of the two men shows Laurier sitting slumped in a chair, looking tired and deflated. The life seems to have gone out of the old man, while behind him Mackenzie King looks confident and complacent as if aware that his time will come. Even by 1916 Laurier felt that he had lived too long and outlived Liberalism. Still, at the end of the war, although tired and ill, he strove to rebuild the Liberal party, which he believed to be Canada's only hope for unity and prosperity.

A heart attack killed Laurier on 18 February 1919. He died holding Zoë's hand, and his last words could well serve as an epitaph for his golden era – 'C'est fini.'

THE RELUCTANT PRIME MINISTER

The Rt Hon Sir

ROBERT LAIRD BORDEN

10 October 1911 – 10 July 1920

The Conservative party . . . carries no indelible imprint from the man who for nearly a quarter of a century led it. He led it by going alongside. He was not a great partisan. He had no overwhelming and audacious bigotries.

AUGUST BRIDLE on Robert Borden in *Masques of Ottawa* (1921)

In 1927 *Maclean's* magazine asked its readers to name the greatest living Canadian. Robert Laird Borden, Canada's eighth Prime Minister, came third on the list after two scientists – Frederick Banting, who discovered insulin, and Charles Saunders, who developed Marquis wheat.

Borden lacked Laurier's charm and charisma. A shy man, patient and plodding, he reluctantly took over the leadership of the Conservative party in 1901 and became Prime Minister 10 years later. Born at Grand Pré, Nova Scotia, in June 1854, Borden recalled with affection the 'distant meadows and quiet village streets of his youth.' A photograph of his father, Andrew, shows a sleepy-eyed man, his features almost lost in the white of his beard and hair. Borden's mother, Eunice, a schoolmaster's daughter, stares confidently out of the frame of her photograph with large, expressive eyes. She seems to have been the main influence in his life. Andrew Borden failed in business and became a station master at Grand Pré. He gave his son a lifelong love of literature and young Robert grew up reading Shakespeare, Dickens and Macauley, and working on the family farm. He also had to contribute to the family income, and at 14 taught classics and mathematics at a local school. Then he headed for the United States to become an assistant master at Glenwood Institute in Matawan, New Jersey. The next year he returned to Halifax and a career in law. After articling for three years, Borden came first in the Nova Scotia bar examinations in 1877. He joined the firm of Graham and Tupper five years later as a junior partner, building up an extensive law practice and carrying cases to the Supreme Court of Canada in Ottawa. In 1889 Borden married Laura Bond, and remained devoted to her throughout their married life, which was childless.

As the nineteenth century drew to a close, Robert Borden seemed settled in the life of a successful Halifax lawyer. With the largest practice in the Maritimes, he earned up to $30,000 a year at a time when a labourer's annual income came to $300. Then Sir Charles Tupper lured Borden into politics, and he stood for Parliament in 1896. Borden won a seat in Halifax, and stood out on the Opposition benches because of his dignified appearance and strong legal reputation. Few photographs show Borden smiling, but those that do reveal generous

Below: *Robert Laird Borden, Canada's eighth Prime Minister, with his Cabinet in 1911. (Borden is eighth from left).*

laugh lines around the eyes, which have a gentle gleam in even his most solemn pictures.

Borden soon became disenchanted with political life. Laura stayed behind in Halifax when he went to Ottawa, and in 1896 he wrote to her that he found political life was 'most stale and flat and unprofitable.' He was convinced that 'it is absolutely unsuited to a man of my temperament and the sooner I get out of it the better.'

That theme would sound throughout Borden's political life. He ran again in the 1900 election and won. Sir Charles Tupper, the Conservative leader, lost his seat and Borden succeeded him on 5 February 1901, a time when, in Borden's words, '. . . the Conservative party was at the nadir of its fortunes and Sir Wilfrid Laurier was then approaching the zenith of his power and influence.' Yet the patient plodding of this political tortoise eventually eclipsed the Liberal hares.

The Liberals, grown slack and complacent during the boom years, had no policies. Borden concentrated his efforts on developing sound foundations for his party's return to power, travelling to the West in 1902 and to the Maritimes in the following year.

Above: *Robert Borden in 1901 when he was a member of Parliament from Nova Scotia and leader of the Conservative Party.*

Left: *Henri Bourassa, a leading proponent of French-Canadian nationalism in the early twentieth century.*

Above: *The closing of Parliament in 1914, showing Centre Block in Ottawa.*

Right: *Prime Minister Borden with Winston Churchill, then Lord of the Admiralty, leaving the Admiralty offices in London, 1914.*

His party lost the election in 1904. On 20 August 1907 Borden outlined a 16-point platform calling for honest elections, Senate reform, advancement by merit in the civil service, free rural mail delivery and state ownership of telephones and telegraphs. Borden used the word 'progressive' to describe his thinking and, in fact, was Canada's first modern-minded Prime Minister. His writings on conservation stressed that development should not be 'destruction and waste' but 'of such a character as to transmit to future generations a continuing heritage.' The Liberals took Borden's ideas and used them as their agendas for reform. Laurier's government established the Civil Service Commission in 1908, the year in which the Liberals returned to power. In the following year Laurier introduced free rural mail delivery and set up a Commission of Conservation.

Laurier's sunny ways proved increasingly inadequate for dealing with the tensions of change. As people in Québec flocked to the cities and the factories, French Canadians, led by Henri Bourassa, feared the loss of their separate identity. When Laurier negotiated free trade with the United States, key Liberals deserted the party. For Borden, reciprocity pointed the way to Canada becoming a mere appendage of the United States. When Laurier called an election for 21 September 1911, Borden presented voters with a choice between 'Canadianism' and 'Continentalism.' He saw Canada, with her 'youthful vitality,' placing herself 'in the highest position within this mighty Empire.'

When the Conservatives won the election, Borden built his Cabinet by inviting representation from Ontario Tories, Québec nationalists and rebel Liberals. His government began to intervene in the economy, regulating the grain trade, acquiring and running grain elevators and providing funds for education in agriculture. Borden also strove to stamp out patronage in government, and introduced bills to create a network of roads and to regulate tariffs. The Liberal Senate rejected these bills, as well as one proposed by Borden to provide funds to Britain to build warships.

When Britain and France went to war with Germany in August 1914, patriotism swept Canada and thousands rushed to recruiting offices. Few

Below: *The first contingent of Canadian expeditionary forces arriving at Plymouth, England, October 1914.*

Right: *Major W A 'Billy' Bishop from Owen Town, Ontario, who became World War I's leading Allied air fighter.*

French Canadians showed much enthusiasm for Britain's cause, and most of the first volunteers consisted of recent British immigrants and the unemployed. The first contingent of the Canadian Expeditionary Force reached England in October 1914.

The British government had not consulted Canada when it declared war on Germany on behalf of the British Empire. Nor did it bother to keep Borden informed of the progress of the war as the casualty lists in Canadian papers lengthened. In the summer of 1915 Borden told Bonar Law, a Canadian member of the British Cabinet: 'Unless I obtain reasonable information ... I shall not advise my countrymen to put further effort into winning the war.' In June he visited 53 English and French hospitals and came away impressed by the suffering and the spirit of wounded Canadians. Borden had begun to realize the price of being part of a mighty empire.

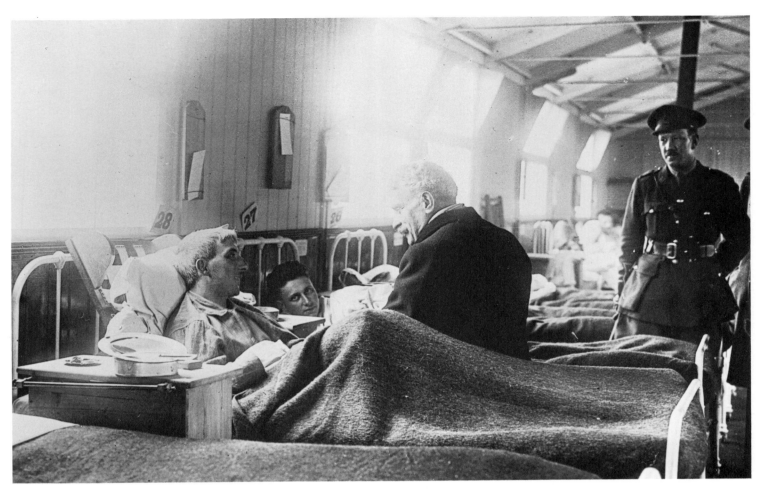

Above: *Premier Sir Robert Borden chats with a wounded soldier at a base hospital on the Western Front in March 1917. The desire of Canadian troops to fight together as a separate corps exacted heavy casualties among them.*

Far right, top: *A Canadian Battalion marches past Sir Robert Borden near the Western Front in July 1918. A Canadian gun fired the last shot of the war a few months later.*

Right: *The 22nd Battalion resting in a shell hole on their way to the front line in September 1917.*

THIS IS NO TIME FOR **PARTY**

VOTE - UNION - GOVERNMENT

Left: *The Ottawa government urged the Canadian soldiers in France to vote in the 1917 Dominion Elections.*

Above: *A plea for non-partisanship in the war effort.*

Above: *Members of the Imperial Munitions Board inspect a cartridge company in Hamilton, Ontario. By 1917 as many as 250,000 workers were producing munitions in Canada.*

In his New Year Message of 1916 Borden pledged to supply half a million soldiers from Canada's population of eight million. Energetic recruiting drives brought in 330,000 volunteers. Canada's battle-hardened troops, fighting together for the first time at Vimy Ridge in northern France on 9 April 1917, Easter Monday, captured the German positions in a day – at a cost of 10,000 dead and wounded. Then the Canadian Corps took part in the disastrous British offensive at Passchendaele, suffering 15,654 casualties; among them was Borden's cousin Robert.

In December 1916 British Prime Minister Lloyd George had set up a War Cabinet on which Borden and others sat as equals. In the spring of 1917, the Canadian Prime Minister created a Union government of Conservatives, Liberals and independents to blend all the talents available to prosecute the war. He also decided to introduce conscription, and took his government to the country in October. On 1 January 1918 the Union government, with 153 seats to the Liberals' 82, put into effect the Military Service Act, but it provided so many exemptions that only a few thousand Canadians were conscripted.

In the spring of 1918 the Germans launched a major offensive on the Western Front. As the Allies retreated, Lloyd George called a meeting of the Imperial War Cabinet on a Sunday afternoon in July. Borden pointed his finger at the British Prime Minister and in a voice shaking with emotion told him that if there was a repetition of Passchendaele 'not a Canadian soldier will leave the shores of Canada . . .' The German offensive faltered in the summer, and the Canadian Corps distinguished itself driving back the enemy to Mons, where the war ended on 11 November 1918. By that time the Canadian dead totalled 69,661, or 10 percent of all who had served.

At home the war transformed Canadian society. Women took on new tasks. When the country went to war Borden's government introduced the Emergency War Measures Act, giving it dictatorial powers. By 1915 military spending equalled the entire government expenditure of 1913. Canadians lent money to the government, which introduced the Wartime Business Profits Tax in 1916. In the following years Borden introduced income tax, on a

Left: *The French steamer,* Mont Blanc, *carrying a cargo of explosives for the war, collided with another ship in Halifax Harbour, generating a disaster that killed 2000 people and leveled buildings along the shore.*

'temporary' basis. By 1917 as many as 250,000 workers were producing munitions in Canada, but runaway inflation eroded wages and food and fuel began to run short. Discontent rose in the cities and the western governments began to fear a rising of the kind that took place in Russia in 1917.

Canada's sacrifice on the battlefield changed Canadians' perception of their place in the Empire. At the Imperial War Conference in 1917, Borden had argued forcibly that Canada and the other former colonies should be recognized as 'autonomous nations of an Imperial Commonwealth.' As head of the Canadian delegation at the Peace Conference in Paris in 1919, the Prime Minister gained international recognition for his country as a self-governing nation. He noted that he 'would be very happy to return to Canada were it not for politics.'

The discontent over high tariffs, tight credit and high cost of living that had simmered in Canada through the last years of the war exploded in the Winnipeg general strike in May 1919. The police repressed it, and when Borden came home from the Paris Peace Conference on 26 May 1919, he knew it was time to quit politics. He resigned in 1920, and Arthur Meighen became Prime Minister.

Borden spent the rest of his days in Ottawa, lecturing, writing, advising politicians, reading poetry, gardening and watching birds. All through his life he suffered from insomnia, indigestion, boils, sciatica and arthritis, but at 80 he still slept outdoors in good weather. He never lost his sense of wonder at simple things like the beauty of the sky. A few hours before this remarkable Canadian died, Borden said to his nephew, 'Remember, Henry, none of this Sir "stuff" at the cemetery, just plain "Robert Laird Borden, born Grand Pré, NS – 1954; died Ottawa, Ontario – 1937."' And so reads his tombstone in Ottawa's Beechwood Cemetery.

Below: *Imperial War Council in London in 1917 attended by Prime Minister Borden (seated, fourth from left), with, among others, General Jan Christian Smuts, later Prime Minister of South Africa, and Sir George Halsey Perley, High Commissioner for Canada in London 1914-22.*

THE FIRST SWORDSMAN OF PARLIAMENT

The Rt Hon
ARTHUR MEIGHEN

10 July 1920 – 29 December 1921

29 June 1926 – 25 September 1926

... Meighen won all the debates, King won all the elections.

ROGER GRAHAM, *Arthur Meighen* (1965)

Above: *Lord (Julian Hedworth George) Byng, who commanded Canadian troops with distinction at Vimy Ridge in 1917 and served as Governor-General of Canada from 1921 to 1926.*

When Arthur Meighen became Unionist Prime Minister in July 1920, Mackenzie King, the Liberal leader, wrote in his diary: 'It is too good to be true.' King had been at university with Meighen and knew the brilliant man's weaknesses. These two men, who became opponents in the House of Commons, offer a sharp contrast in how a Canadian Prime Minister can win and lose power.

Born in June 1874, Meighen grew up on a hard-scrabble farm in Anderson, Ontario. His parents' Presbyterianism imbued him with the virtues of hard work, dedication and seriousness of purpose. He once admitted that he had never told a funny story in his life. In school Meighen became an effective debater, but when he enrolled at the University of Toronto in 1892, he took mathematics. After graduation Meighen trained as a teacher and taught in a small Ontario town. He resigned his position after a quarrel with the school board, and went west to make his fortune. Like Borden, Meighen had tired of teaching and articled as a lawyer, settling in Portage La Prairie, Manitoba, in 1900.

Tall, handsome, aloof, with deep-set eyes and a soulful look, Meighen had a wonderful way with words and soon attracted the attention of politicians.

He stood for the Conservatives in 1908. The party lost the election, but Meighen won his seat and soon began to stand out in the Opposition. The *Manitoba Free Press* called him 'the first swordsman of Parliament.' Meighen rushed into debates as if going to battle, cutting and thrusting with an acid tongue that diminished his opponents. 'I am always happier facing an audience that has to be convinced,' he once wrote.

When the Conservatives came to power in 1911, Borden recognized that Meighen's debating talents might prove a political liability. The new Prime Minister sought to win over enemies by compromise and kindness, but he soon found that he had need of Meighen's skills and intelligence. When the Liberals frustrated Borden's attempts to provide money for Britain's battleships, Meighen suggested the use of closure to end debate in the House of Commons. In June 1913 Meighen became Solicitor-General. In the following years, the war provided exceptional scope for his talents. He nationalized the Grand Trunk Pacific and the Canadian Northern Railway, creating the basis of the Canadian National Railways. He also brought down the Military Service Act, which introduced conscription, and presented the Wartime Elections Bill, which removed the vote from thousands of Canadians of German origin. In 1919 Meighen went out west to settle the Winnipeg strike, and he consistently defended the policy of high tariffs that irritated farmers.

When Robert Borden resigned in 1920, burned out by the stress of war, it took the Conservatives only a week to elect Meighen as his successor. At 46 he became Canada's youngest Prime Minister to that date. However, his shining mind could not grasp the realities of life at the top. He called an election for December 1921, campaigning on the 'Old Policy' of high tariffs. For the first time three major parties fielded candidates. Thomas Crerar led the Progressives, a farmer-based party that won 65 seats. The Liberals took all the seats in Québec and had 115 places in the House of Commons. When the Conservatives won in 50 ridings and Meighen lost his seat, he found another one and rebuilt his party.

In 1922 Britain almost went to war with Turkey when nationalists pinned British troops down in the port of Chanak. Mackenzie King refused to back the mother country by providing soldiers, but Meighen left no doubts as to where his loyalties lay. In

Right: *The sea of troubles facing Meighen as head of state was stormy.*

Toronto he said: 'When Britain's message came then Canada should have said "Ready, aye, ready; we stand by you."' Meighen never hesitated to say where he stood, while King avoided doing so whenever possible. In the 1925 election the Conservatives took 116 seats, and although the Liberals held 101, King lost his seat. The Progressives took only 24 seats, and King retained power with their co-operation. Then a scandal erupted in the Customs Department after senior officials had become involved in bootlegging to meet the needs of thirsty Americans suffering during Prohibition. As a result King asked Governor-General Lord Byng to dissolve Parliament.

Instead Byng asked Arthur Meighen to form a government, and gave King a chance to play the outraged politician. The 'King-Byng Thing' wrecked the careers of Meighen and Byng. In those days, MPs appointed to posts in the Cabinet had to resign and run for re-election. In taking over the government, Meighen appointed ministers 'without portfolio' who acted as ministers for their departments. They did not have to resign, but he did. King attacked the actions of Lord Byng and the constitutionality of Meighen's way of appointing his ministers. On 2 July 1926 the Meighen government fell. King, happy to have issues to obscure the customs scandal, won the election. Meighen lost his seat and left politics to join a Toronto investment firm. In his new life he made new friends. The poet E J Pratt recalled how Meighen played golf, which showed that old habits died hard. The former Prime Minister treated the pin like an opponent, Pratt noted, 'which had to be out-manoeuvred, not so much reached as attacked.'

In 1932 Prime Minister Bennett appointed Meighen to the Senate and made him Government Leader there in the hope that he would help the country cope with the Depression. Meighen could do little, but in 1941 the Conservatives asked him to lead them again. Resigning his Senate seat, Meighen ran in the election in February 1942, only to lose to the candidate of the Co-operative Commonwealth Federation, a teacher named Joseph Noseworthy.

At the Conservative leadership convention in Winnipeg in 1943, Meighen handed over his post to John Bracken, Premier of Manitoba, and the party added Progressive to its name. Meighen told the audience: 'Gentlemen, I am through. . . . Fortune came and fortune fled; believe in my sincerity when I say that I see no reason for sympathy.' Meighen lived to see the Conservatives under John Diefenbaker win the 1957 election, and he died in his sleep in Toronto on 4 August 1960.

Above: *As Senate leader in 1932 Meighen could do little to cope with the Depression. He is shown here in conference with Richard Bennett, who, as Prime Minister, appointed Meighen to the Senate.*

Left: *When Arthur Meighen gave up the Conservative leadership in 1943, he told the audience '. . . believe in my sincerity when I say that I see no reason for sympathy.'*

THE MILLIONAIRE PRIME MINISTER

The Rt Hon

RICHARD BEDFORD BENNETT

7 August 1930 – 23 October 1935

Bennett is clever, well-informed, has a remarkable memory. . . . He is contemptuous of the intelligence and efforts of others — in every respect a lone wolf. . . .

GEORGE BLACK, Yukon MP (1940)

Right: *Richard Bedford Bennett, 'Dickie' to his family and friends, worked and studied hard as a boy growing up on a small farm in Hopewell Hill, New Brunswick.*

In March 1932, during the depths of the Depression, Prime Minister Richard Bennett agreed to meet with a delegation of the un-employed in Ottawa. As an armoured car sat on Parliament Hill, armed Mounties patrolled government buildings and a mounted troop hid behind the Centre Block, Bennett must have wondered why these poor people had fallen from grace. His own life showed how clean living and hard work could lead to financial and political success.

Born in 1870 at Hopewell Hill, New Brunswick, 'Dickie' came from a family of shipbuilders. His father drank, the business declined as the era of wooden ships ended and the family struggled to earn a living from their small farm. Young Bennett worked and studied hard, graduating as a teacher at 16. He had a quick tongue and a temper to match, but soon became a school principal. At 19 he met

Max Aitken, the future Lord Beaverbrook, who became a lifelong friend. Aitken recalled that Bennett was wearing 'a bowler hat a bit too big for him' and had a reputation for 'rectitude and godliness.' Bennett left teaching for the law in 1890, and graduated from Dalhousie University in Halifax three years later. Then he joined a law firm in Chatham, New Brunswick.

A handsome, tall, courteous man, Bennett wooed several women, but remained a bachelor all his life. He also had a passion for chocolates. In 1896 he moved to Calgary to work for Senator James Lougheed, one of the busiest lawyers in the West. Here he lived in a hotel and centred his life around the Methodist church. Bennett never owned a permanent home until he retired from politics and moved to England, where he bought Juniper Hill, near London.

In Calgary the young lawyer dressed formally in top hat, wing collar and morning coat, eating huge meals to put on weight to impress people. He soon became a leading lawyer in the West, acting as counsel for the Canadian Pacific Railway and the Hudson's Bay Company. Bennett had a tough, tenacious mind, astonishing Max Aitken with 'his grasp of details, sound judgement and swift decision.' By 1914 the lawyer-businessman earned around $65,000 a year at a time when a skilled labourer in Calgary received about $3 a day. Aitken offered Bennett a chance to invest in a number of business ventures, and Bennett invited Aitken to join him in raising capital for Alberta Pacific Grain Elevators. By 1918 this venture alone provided Bennett with an income of $33,750 annually.

Bennett won a seat on the Legislative Council of the Northwest Territories in 1898, but failed in his bid for a place in the House of Commons in 1900. In 1909, four years after Alberta became a province, Bennett won a seat in the Provincial Legislature. He then ran for the federal Conservatives in 1911, praising the Empire, temperance, the CPR, hard

work and ambition. He took the riding, but soon became bored in Ottawa, writing to Max Aitken in England that there was little to do and that he was 'sick of it here.' During World War I Borden put him to work using his talents for organizing manpower.

Bennett lost his seat in the 1921 election, and returned to law and business in Calgary. He sold his interest in the grain elevators for a capital gain of $1.35 million, and inherited control of the E B Eddy Company in Hull when two friends died. Persuaded to run in the 1925 election, Bennett took the Calgary seat only to see Arthur Meighen outmanoeuvred and

defeated during the 'King-Byng Thing'. In 1927 Bennett became Conservative leader and poured money and energy into the party. His opportunity for leadership came just after the Depression began. King's government balanced its budget, but the provinces demanded aid to deal with rising unemployment. On 3 April 1930, the Prime Minister declared in the House of Commons that the federal government would 'not give to any Tory government for their alleged unemployment purposes . . . a five-cent piece.' Those words haunted King during the 1930 election, as people threw five-cent pieces onto the platform whenever he spoke.

Bennett thought the solution to unemployment problems lay in tariff reform, and promised to 'blast a way into markets that have been closed,' adding that his government would initiate whatever action was needed to end unemployment 'or perish in the attempt.' Wearing a plug hat, tail coat, striped trousers and well-shined shoes, the Prime Minister looked like a parody of a capitalist millionaire. He had poured $600,000 of his own money into the election campaign. If such a man could not rescue Canada from the Depression, who could?

When he became Prime Minister, Bennett retained the portfolios of Finance and External Affairs, and drafted all the major bills himself. An Ottawa story told of Bennett walking around, talking to himself. A visitor asked what he was doing and the reply came, 'He's holding a Cabinet meeting.' Bennett hoped that tight money, fiscal restraint and high tariffs would stem the Depression. As it deepened he called a conference in 1932 on the theme of Imperial Preference for Goods. Bennett also asked Parliament for $20 million to employ men on public works such as restoring the Halifax Citadel. When No 1 Northern Wheat, the best grade, fell to 50 cents a bushel, Bennett met the crisis in the traditional Canadian way by setting up a Royal Commission. When drought hit the Prairies, and fields and family funds dried up, farmers hitched

Above: *Prime Minister Bennett, surrounded by members of his Cabinet, speaking over the Transatlantic Telephone to Sir George Perley at the British Empire Trade Fair in Buenos Aires 13 March 1931.*

Top, left: *William Maxwell Aitken, later Lord Beaverbrook, a lifelong friend of Richard Bennett and an outstanding example of young men from the Maritimes who worked their way to positions of distinction.*

Left: *Richard Bennett as a young lawyer in Calgary, Alberta, in 1912. Even then he always wore the tall top hat that was later to characterize him.*

Right: *A poor farm family in front of their log shack on the Prairies during the lean years of the Depression.*

Below: *Lacking the money for gasoline, Depression-poor Prairie farmers hitched their cars to teams of horses. The practice gave rise to the term 'Bennett Buggy' after Prime Minister Bennett.*

horses to their gasless automobiles to create 'Bennett buggies.'

The Prime Minister sought ways to solve unemployment. The government set up camps where single unemployed men could receive room, board and 20 cents a day while working on government projects. Legislation set up bodies to organize marketing boards, reduce mortgage payments and establish the Bank of Canada. Bennett's government also created the Canadian Radio Broadcasting Corporation. The Prime Minister received hundreds of letters from desperate people. He ensured that all were answered and sent along a few dollars to those in need. On Thanksgiving Day, 1934, Bennett spoke to Canadians from London, England, telling them that they should be thankful 'for the manifold blessings that Providence has bestowed on them.'

Then, quite suddenly, Bennett ceased to rely on personal kindness and exhortations, and reversed his approach to unemployment. Without telling his Cabinet, he introduced a new series of measures to deal with the crisis. Borrowed from Roosevelt's New Deal in the United States, they included the 48-Hour Week Bill, the Weekly Day of Rest Bill and the Minimum Wages Bill as well as the Employment and Social Insurance Bill. The unemployed from the West marched on Ottawa and clashed with police in Regina in June 1935. When the country went to the polls in that year, the Liberals offered voters a choice, 'King or Chaos.' King led his party back to power with 178 seats. Bennett stayed on to lead the Conservatives, but neither the reformers nor the old guard found him acceptable, and his health began to decline. In July 1938 Bennett left politics and sailed

Left: *Camp huts in a relief project in Barriefield, Ontario, April 1934.*

Right: *Relief kitchens were set up in an effort to alleviate the desperation of hunger in the thirties. This one shows a line-up in Edmonton.*

Left: *A destitute family returns to Saskatoon in June 1934 after a hopeless effort to find employment.*

Right: *Prime Minister Bennett departs aboard the* Empress of Australia *to attend the Imperial Conference in England in 1930.*

for England, where he had bought an estate next to Lord Beaverbrook's. At Juniper Hill he found a new interest – gardening. He also planted and consumed large quantities of asparagus. Lord Beaverbrook secured a peerage for his friend in 1941, and the

poor boy from New Brunswick became Viscount Bennett of Mickleham, Calgary and Hopewell. Then he developed diabetes.

On 26 June 1947 the former Prime Minister of Canada went to London. He returned in the late afternoon, and walked with his dog Bill in the garden on a very hot evening. Lord Beaverbrook dropped in to see him, finding him 'depressed and despondent.' Bennett refused his friend's invitation to 'a quiet but gay dinner with good soup and plenty of asparagus.' Instead, Bennett dined alone, then sat in his library looking out of the window. Undressing with the help of his valet, Bennett decided to take a

Below: *Protest by the unemployed at the Parliament Building in Edmonton in February 1929.*

Above: *The working class felt that Bennett, in his top hat and striped trousers, lacked rapport with the common man and his problems.*

Left: *Citizens of Regina and transient unemployed riot in the market square on 1 July 1935.*

bath, but first he read his Bible. On the following morning, his valet found Bennett's body in the overflowing bath. He had died of a heart attack.

As Beaverbrook noted, two Church of England bishops and the General of the Salvation Army attended Bennett's funeral on 30 June, but 'I did not see a Methodist minister in the company of the mourners.' The former Prime Minister, who is buried in the churchyard at Mickleham, left an estate valued at $3.5 million. A lifelong resident of the village told a visiting Canadian journalist in the 1980s: 'I don't know what you did to Bennett over there in Canada. . . . He was a much-loved figure in this area.'

THE INCREDIBLE CANADIAN

The Rt Hon

WILLIAM LYON MACKENZIE KING

29 December 1921 – 28 July 1926

25 September 1926 – 6 August 1930

23 October 1935 – 15 November 1948

We had no shape
Because he never took sides,
And no sides
Because he never allowed them
to take shape.

F R SCOTT, 'W.L.M.K.' (1957)

During a visit to Switzerland in 1900 Mackenzie King stayed in a small hotel high in the mountains. He watched the sun set on a Saturday evening, judging it 'extremely fine.' Below the hotel a man and two women worked frantically in the moonlight, cutting and turning the hay before Sunday came. King asked for a fork and helped them in their work. 'It was idyllic,' he wrote in his diary. 'For once I felt myself a god and life a myth.' After breaking bread and drinking beer with his fellow workers, King returned to his hotel, knelt and 'prayed to the God of Nature and the world to make me pure and strong.' On that night King slipped across the boundaries of convention and became a worker with others, losing himself in a communal task and experiencing 'a night that will live with me for ever.'

This anecdote reveals a great deal about the character of Canada's tenth Prime Minister, who was a bit of a mystic as well as a realist. Essentially a repressed Victorian romantic, King became imbued with a knightly spirit through reading Tennyson's *Idylls of the King*. In the year after his experience in Switzerland, when King's dearest friend, Arthur

Below: *Boyhood home of Mackenzie King in Berlin (now Kitchener,) Ontario.*

Left: *Mackenzie King at the age of two in Berlin, Ontario.*

Above: *Mrs. John King (née Grace Mackenzie), mother of Canada's eleventh Prime Minister.*

Harper, died in a vain attempt to save a drowning woman, King had a statue of Galahad erected in front of the Parliament Buildings in Ottawa to commemorate him. On its base are Tennyson's words: 'Galahad . . . Cried, If I lose myself, I save myself!'

Instead of boldly seeking dragons to slay, King tried to tackle the problems of society in a cautious way. William Lyon Mackenzie, his maternal grandfather after whom he was named, led the 1837 rebellion against colonial rule and the Family Compact in Upper Canada. King felt compelled to fulfill his grandfather's destiny. While Mackenzie was in exile in the United States, King's mother, Isabel Grace, lived in poverty. An ambitious woman, she dominated King, even after her death in 1917. King's paternal grandfather, however, had been a British bombardier who helped to quell the 1837 rebellion. Thus King inherited a tradition of rebellion – and one of repression.

His lawyer-father, John King, settled in Berlin (now Kitchener), Ontario, in 1869, and here William was born in December 1874. Young Willie grew up in a comfortable, close-knit, middle-class family. His father prospered in Berlin, but did less well when he moved to Toronto in 1893. Mackenzie King had to help to support the family as its fortunes ebbed, and consequently developed an obsession about money. After entering the University of Toronto in 1891, King took an active part in sports, debates and politics while gaining three degrees. He even

Below: *King as Minister of Labour in 1910.*

Right: *A Liberal to the core, King had a tendency to avoid taking strong stands on controversial issues, which made him seem to agree with everyone.*

organized a protest against a professor, and earned the nickname 'Rex.' King also did good works among the unfortunate victims of society, reading to patients at the Hospital for Sick Children and trying to stop prostitutes from plying their trade. While in Chicago doing graduate work in 1896, King lived in a settlement house and did social work among slum dwellers. Then he went to Harvard University, travelling to Europe on a fellowship in 1899.

In the meantime in Canada, Laurier's Liberal government was taking some steps to alleviate the increasingly obvious exploitation of Canadian workers. Laurier believed that a factual publication would help labour and management understand each other, so he cabled King in Rome, offering him a government job in Canada and he came home to start the *Labour Gazette*. King had investigated the sweat shops of the Toronto garment trade in 1897 and had written newspaper articles about the conditions. The articles had caught the eye of Postmaster-General William Mulock, a family friend, who had commissioned a report from King on the garment industry; it was he who suggested him as editor of the *Labour Gazette*. As King confided to his diary, what followed 'reads like a fairy tale.' Within days of arriving in Ottawa in July 1900, he found himself elevated to Deputy Minister of a new Department of Labour. An effective and energetic civil servant, King moved across Canada settling industrial disputes. In 1905 Governor-General Lord Grey called him 'the Peace Maker.' King soon sought the help of Laurier to enter politics, and he ran for Parliament in 1908, becoming a Privy Councillor and Minister of Labour when elected. He joined a worn-out government, and lost his seat when the Liberals fell from power in 1911.

For a while King found casual employment, and then joined the Rockefeller Foundation as head of

Industrial Relations to undertake research at $12,000 a year in 1914. Instead of working as a researcher, he went to Colorado to settle a bloody strike at John D Rockefeller's copper mines, where he persuaded the miners – and Rockefeller – to accept a company union. During the Conscription Crisis of 1917, King left the bedside of his dying mother to run for a seat in North York, a constituency associated with his grandfather. He lost, but proved his devotion to Laurier and the Liberals, which stood him in good stead in later years.

King's book, *Industry and Humanity*, setting out his approach to creating industrial democracy, appeared in 1918, and has been described by one historian as 'almost unreadable, written in muddy prose and full of soppy moralism.' At the 1919 Liberal leadership, however, King's enlightened ideas, skills as a conciliator, anti-conscription stance and loyalty to Laurier made him the natural choice for party leader. While campaigning for the 1921 election, he did not take a stand on issues. As he later told a reporter, he believed it was a great mistake for a political party to define policy in detail and 'give the other fellows a target to shoot at.' When the Conservatives lost that election, King became Prime Minister in a minority government.

In office, King tried to absorb the Progressives, who held 65 seats, and to keep the Liberal party in the middle road so as to appeal to all Canadians. However, he did take a firm stand on relations with Britain, refusing to send troops to Turkey during the Chanak Crisis in 1922 and opposing the idea of a uniform foreign policy for the Commonwealth in 1923. In 1926 King attended the Imperial Conference that redefined the status of the dominions and paved the way for the Statute of Westminster in 1931, which made them equal with Britain.

Bruce Hutchinson, dean of Canadian journalists, met King in 1925. At age 50 the Prime Minister was a 'brisk, cheerful, twinkling man . . . short, corpulent, and bald with a single wisp of damp hair plastered across his forehead' and clad in 'an antique suit.' He had the 'hands of a physician . . . as delicate and soft as a woman's.' King talked at length with the young reporter, for as Hutchinson put it, 'No stone of politics was too small for King to turn in an election year, no potential supporter too insignificant to be baited with favours and glued with birdlime.' It's little wonder that the writer called his biography of Mackenzie King *The Incredible Canadian*.

King lost power temporarily to Arthur Meighen in 1925, but returned to office in the following year by arousing voters over Governor-General Lord Byng's interference in Canada's political affairs and the way in which Meighen had appointed his ministers. The 1920s, a time of mild prosperity, provided the ideal climate for King's cautious brand of administration. He introduced old age pensions in 1927 in co-operation with those provinces interested in implementing the scheme. He based receipt of the $20 monthly pension cheque on a means test.

Left: *Prime Minister King in Privy Council Chamber with his Cabinet in 1930.*

Mackenzie King had the good luck to lose the election of July 1930 to Richard Bennett's Conservatives, and the full weight of the Depression fell upon the new administration. When King came back as Prime Minister in 1935, economic conditions had begun to improve slightly. In office King learned how to obscure issues with what one historian calls a 'mist of words.' The Prime Minister simply closed his eyes and his ears to unpleasant matters. After meeting Adolf Hitler in 1937, King concluded that the German dictator was 'a man of deep sincerity and a genuine patriot' who sought only peace, but he also informed Hitler that if Britain went to war with Germany, Canada would fight with Britain.

Seven days after Britain declared war on Germany in September 1939, the Canadian Parliament followed suit, with a promise by the government that there would be no conscription. King soon found himself being accused of doing too little for the war effort by Mitchell Hepburn, Premier of Ontario, and of doing too much by Maurice Duplessis, his counterpart in Québec, who feared Ottawa's encroachment on his autonomy. So King went to the country in March 1940 and received the largest majority of any Canadian government to that time.

Then came the attack on Belgium, Holland and France by German panzers, which swiftly swamped the Allied armies and drove them into the sea at Dunkirk. King had around him an exceptionally talented group of men including Ministers of Defence J L Ralston and Angus L Macdonald, and Minister of Munitions and Supply C D Howe. After Dunkirk the country geared itself for a total war effort, expanding its armed forces and industrial production. King initially decided against conscription since the three services had recruited thousands of men, some of whom were patriots,

THIS IS OUR STRENGTH

LABOUR and MANAGEMENT

are pooling their strength to give us the means for victory in war··and progress in peace.

Left: *During the Second World War labour and management joined forces in an all-out and heroic effort.*

Right: *A five-year-old boy says goodbye to his father, leaving for active service in Europe during Second World War.*

Far right: *Canadian soldiers returning to England after the German army crushed France in 1940. English women welcome them with the Union Jack.*

Below: *The First Canadian Division in England departs for the fighting in France.*

Below, far right: *The Angus shops of the Canadian Railway Pacific in Montreal, 1941, rolling out tanks they produced for the war in Europe.*

others of whom had been too long without work.

In December 1941 the 2000 members of a Canadian force rushed to protect Hong Kong were killed or captured by the Japanese. In April 1942 King's government organized a plebiscite to sound out Canadians on their attitude towards ordering volunteers in the forces overseas. In his oblique and tortuous way, King proposed 'not necessarily conscription, but conscription if necessary' as a way of handling the problem of making sure the generals had enough soldiers. He received overwhelming support for his policy, but 72.9 percent of the people of Québec refused to endorse it. King had always paid careful attention to Québec, with the help of Ernest Lapointe, Minister of Justice and a trusted adviser. When Lapointe died in 1941, King had recruited Louis St Laurent, a respected Québec lawyer, who backed his stand on conscription.

In August 1942 Canada suffered 2700 casualties, killed or captured during the abortive raid on Dieppe. In the following year Canadian troops took part in the invasion of Sicily and then began to fight their way up the Italian peninsula, where casualties among the infantry were again heavy. In June 1944 the Allies invaded France, and the Canadian infantry suffered more massive casualties, increasing pressure in English Canada to send men conscripted for home service into battle. In October Ralston went overseas where, like Borden, he saw at first hand the sufferings of front-line soldiers. He came back convinced that conscripts should be sent into action, but King forced his resignation and replaced him with General A G L McNaughton as Minister of Defence. McNaughton, a popular soldier, claimed that he could secure volunteers to fight in Europe. He failed to do so, and King, faced with a generals' revolt, finally agreed to send 15,000 conscripts to fight overseas. Only about 2500 of them actually reached the front lines by 1945, as the war ended.

King had distrusted British Prime Minister Winston Churchill as an imperialist, but during the war he became friendly with him and with American

Far left: *The battlefield during the disastrous raid on Dieppe in France, August 1942, where Canadian forces suffered heavy casualties.*

Above: *A Canadian-built Hurricane fighter.*

Left: *Canada declared war on Germany only six days after Britain and was as dogged in pursuit of victory.*

Below: *A squad of Canadian soldiers fire a farewell salute over the graves of fifty of their countrymen who gave their lives at Dieppe.*

Three Canadian war vessels seek out a reported enemy submarine in the St Lawrence River.

Inset: *First ship launched at West Coast shipyard in 1942.*

Soldiers of the 9th Canadian Infantry Brigade and the Highland Light Infantry landing in Normandy on D-day, 6 June 1944.

Inset: *President Roosevelt, Prime Minister King, and Prime Minister Churchill at Québec Conference, 1944.*

president Franklin Delano Roosevelt. One day King and Roosevelt were up to their necks in a swimming pool at Warm Springs, 'stark naked except for little belly bands,' as King put it. The President said: 'Mackenzie, what are you and I going to do about the defence of North America?' Out of this casual remark came the Ogdensburg Agreement of 1940 that created a defensive alliance between the two countries. In the following year, Canadian manufacturers began to export large quantities of equipment to the United States, but as Canada's economy became more closely linked to that of America, King worried about the country being absorbed by its southern neighbour. In 1944 when Churchill and Roosevelt met in Québec City, King revelled in his role as mediator between two great powers.

In 1943, however, the Liberal government had lost four bye-elections. Two seats went to the Co-operative Commonwealth Federation (CCF), and two others were lost in Québec. Polls showed the CCF becoming increasingly popular. King ordered a meeting of the Liberal party's National Advisory Council, and castigated his opponents for exploiting popular discontent over wartime controls. Then he laid the foundations for retaining power after the war. Influenced by Keynesian economics and the fear of socialism, the Prime Minister introduced family allowances and unemployment insurance in 1944. The government saw these transfer payments as a way of putting money into circulation when the war ended, the troops came home and the defence industries closed their doors. Thus were laid the foundations of the modern welfare state as King steered his party down the middle of the road, avoiding the excesses of socialism and reactionary conservatism. In June 1945 King went to the country. The Liberal party platform called for 'full employment and maximum production,' a labour code, housing and health programmes, steps to assure

Canadian national sovereignty, and national unity based on 'the partnership of the two great races and respect for the historic rights of minorities.'

The Liberals won the election, but King lost his seat. In 1946 Louis St Laurent became responsible for External Affairs, and King chose him as his successor, annointing him at a convention in August 1948. When Mackenzie King resigned that year, he set a new record for more time in office than any Prime Minister in the British Commonwealth.

King had never married and after he retired he pottered around on his country estate at Kingsmere, north of Ottawa. He died on 22 July 1950, thanking the nurse who attended him with his last words. In recent years, his achievements in office have been reassessed. Many people believe that King will be remembered, in the words of poet F R Scott:

> *Wherever men honour ingenuity,*
> *Ambiguity, inactivity, and political longevity.*

Mackenzie King led 'a very double life,' as he confided to his diary. He learned how to balance the forces that threatened to tear the country apart. He

Left: *Prime Minister King broadcasting his victory message from San Francisco on V-E Day 8 May 1945.*

Below: *V-E Day official parade to Parliament Hill, Ottawa, 8 May 1945.*

Top: *Prime Minister King addressing the Paris Conference of the United Nations in 1946.*

Above: *King congratulates Louis St Laurent on his election as leader of the Liberal Party in 1948.*

did not simply compromise on issues. In Cabinet he arrived at decisions by consensus, listening to each of his ministers before plotting a course of action or deciding not to act. King compared politics to sailing a ship, suggesting that one should 'not try to go straight ahead but reach one's course having regard to the prevailing wind.' He advised Lester Pearson that 'in the course of human history far more has been accomplished for the welfare and progress of mankind in preventing bad actions than in doing good ones.' King disliked dealing with the small details of political life and left them to others. At the same time he showed great sensitivity to the feelings of the average Canadian struggling to make sense of an increasingly confusing world.

He realized, he once said, that there was a real world and an imaginary one. King learned to walk the line between them. At Kingsmere, his country retreat, he built an artificial ruin, a 'folly,' and played the rural squire where civilization ended and the wilderness began. King constantly had to balance his desire to serve others and his personal ambition.

When awarded the Order of Merit, the highest honour that the British bestow, King felt that his little dog, Pat II, deserved it 'a thousand times more' than he did. He hung the award next to the poster offering a thousand-dollar reward for anyone apprehending his rebel grandfather.

While directing the destinies of Canada, Mackenzie King also dabbled in spiritualism. When his dog Pat I died in July 1941, King sang hymns and thought of how he felt 'at dear Mother's side in her last illness.' He gave the dying dog messages of love to take to his family and to Sir Wilfrid and Lady Laurier. It is easy to laugh at such excesses, but they provide a glimpse of the depths of loneliness that King had to endure. The Prime Minister developed an obsessive concern with signs and dates to reassure himself that he was doing the right thing, another indication of an isolated individual who must constantly seek indications that he has some control over the world.

With Mackenzie King's death and the accession of Louis St Laurent, Canada slipped into a new era. The mystic gave way to the managers as the country boomed during the postwar years.

Left: *Mackenzie King with his dog Pat at his country home, Kingsmere.*

Below: *Former Prime Minister King lies in state in the Hall of Fame of the Parliament Buildings in Ottawa, 1950.*

UNCLE LOUIS

The Rt Hon
LOUIS ST LAURENT

15 November 1948 – 21 June 1957

It was said that when St Laurent was at the zenith of his power and prestige that if he were ever defeated there might be regret but no tears or sorrow, and so it was.

C G POWER *A Party Politician* (1966)

At his first Cabinet meeting as Prime Minister in 1948, Louis St Laurent received a cane that had belonged to Sir Wilfrid Laurier. Then he lit a cigarette and other ministers followed suit. His Liberal predecessor Mackenzie King had forbidden smoking in the Council Chamber. After the Cabinet meeting, St Laurent went to his office on the second floor of the East Block and worked until about 8 o'clock. As he left he discovered that the elevator operator was still on duty, waiting to take him down one floor. King had insisted on this, but St Laurent told the man to leave with the rest of the staff in the future. He could walk down one flight of steps just like anyone else!

Louis St Laurent put a human face on the long-lived Liberal government, but he also did more than that. King had no system for organizing his official papers, often arrived late for meetings and appointments, and did not like being disturbed by his ministers and visitors. St Laurent kept regular hours, organized his paperwork, kept in touch with his ministers while letting them run their departments and managed the affairs of Canada with great efficiency. One of his staff said they felt that they were working *with* him rather than *for* him.

Like Sir Robert Borden, St Laurent became Prime Minister most reluctantly. Until Mackenzie King invited him to join his Cabinet in 1941 to replace Ernest Lapointe, St Laurent had no involvement in politics. Born in February 1882 in Compton in Québec's Eastern Townships, he grew up bilingual, speaking English with his mother and French with his father, a merchant. Moïse St Laurent's general store served as a centre of the predominantly Protestant community. As French Canadians trickled into the area, Moïse gave them advice and acted as a bridge between the two language groups. His son learned to read and write in English before going to a French Catholic school. At school Dorilla Têtu, a teacher, recognized his abilities and coached St Laurent so well that he became the first French Canadian from Compton to enter a classical college. St Laurent spent six years in the monastic atmosphere of St Charles Seminary in Sherbrooke, destined for the priesthood. When he graduated in 1902, however, he went to Laval University in Québec City to study law.

The future Prime Minister followed the traditional course of a successful lawyer, although his first position paid only $50 a month. St Laurent had a very persuasive style, summarizing the facts of a case in a calm and objective manner, convincing judges that he had correctly assessed the situation. He set up his own practice, helped to found the Canadian Bar Association, lectured at Laval University, and appeared before the Supreme Court of Canada and the Judicial Committee of the Privy Council in London. He also acted for provincial and federal governments, whereby he gained the reputation of being 'a lawyer's lawyer.'

Below: *Louis St Laurent (left) talks with Mackenzie King, whom he succeeded as Prime Minister.*

Above: *Prime Minister St
Laurent (left) with Viscount
Alexander of Tunis (in
uniform), Governor-General
of Canada, at welcoming
ceremonies for
Newfoundland when it
became a province on 1 April
1949.*

In 1908 Louis St Laurent married Jeanne Renault.
The couple built a large house on Québec City's
Grand Allée and had five children. From 1937 to
1940 St Laurent served as counsel on the Rowell-
Sirois Commission that examined the economic and
financial basis of Confederation. As he travelled
across the country, St Laurent became an articulate
spokesman for Canadian unity, stressing the need
for harmony between the two founding peoples.

By 1941 St Laurent was earning $50,000 a year and
he owned 33 insurance policies. On 4 December in
that year he received a phone call from Mackenzie
King, inviting him to come to Ottawa. St Laurent
knew what King wanted, but did not ask the reason
for the invitation. He travelled to Ottawa on
5 December, and King offered him the post of
Minister of Justice as expected. Two days later the
Japanese attacked Pearl Harbor and on 10 December
St Laurent joined the Cabinet at a salary of $12,000 a
year. He sat at King's right hand, acting as the Prime
Minister's anchor in Québec. St Laurent stressed that
he had joined the government as a 'conscript' for the
duration of the war only. However, King came to rely
increasingly on his new minister, and wrote that the
more he saw of St Laurent 'the nobler soul I believe
him to be.' He described him as 'One of God's
gentlemen if ever there was one . . . so sensible, so
straight and so exceedingly able.'

Disciplined, decisive and dutiful, St Laurent saw
himself as 'just a good average Canadian.' Lean and
trim, he had a handsome ruddy face and a compact
look. A journalist called St Laurent 'a crisp terrier of a
man,' but the man also exuded old world charm and
dignity. He had a calming effect upon King, supporting the war effort and standing by him on the
conscription issue. Shortly after winning a seat in the
House of Commons, the new Minister of Justice
ordered the removal of 20,000 Canadians of Japanese origin from the west coast and the confiscation
of their property.

The Liberals ran – and won – the 1945 election on
the platform of 'not necessarily Mackenzie King, but
Mackenzie King if necessary.' The aging Prime
Minister turned over more and more responsibility
to St Laurent, who longed to return to his family and
his comfortable home on the Grand Allée. In 1946,
however, he became Minister of External Affairs, and
began to see how Canada could play a mediating
role in the postwar world. When the Liberals held a
leadership convention in 1948, St Laurent won on
the first ballot.

So he stayed in Ottawa, becoming Canada's
second French Canadian Prime Minister on 15
November 1948. Then he travelled across the
country, meeting ordinary Canadians. A reporter,
noting his easy rapport with children, dubbed him

'Uncle Louis.' Another journalist, however, noted that both King and St Laurent guarded their privacy. King's thoughts 'slid out of your grasp like jelly' while St Laurent lowered an iron curtain that 'nearly decapitated the questioner as it fell' when anyone probed into unpleasant issues. Behind the affable image of Uncle Louis lay a very tough mind. At ease in both languages and cultures, St Laurent believed that 'the concept of the father of a family was the best one to be applied to the management of public affairs.' St Laurent's paternalism and his common sense suited Canada as the country and its people rode the boom years of the postwar world.

The Prime Minister provided decisive leadership in his early years in power. The Trans-Canada Highway and St Laurent Seaway were initiated, appeals to the British Privy Council were abolished and Vincent Massey was appointed the first Canadian-born Governor-General. St Laurent completed Confederation when he welcomed Newfoundland into Canada in 1949, and he also set up a government department to administer and develop Canada's vast northern territories. The St Laurent government set up the Massey Commission in 1949 to look at arts, letters and sciences in Canada and launched nation-

Right: *Louis St Laurent became his country's second French-Canadian Prime Minister.*

Far right: *The ice-breaker* Ernest Lapointe *was the first ship in history to enter the St Lawrence locks, on 16 April 1959.*

Below: *Construction in 1960 on the Nigel Creek Bridge in Alberta, a segment of the Trans-Canada Highway.*

Below (top): *President Eisenhower, Governor-General Massey, and Prime Minister St Laurent at War Memorial in Ottawa, 1953.*

Below (bottom): *Canadian infantry arriving in Egypt in UN action, 1956.*

wide television. People received an old age pension at 70 without a means test, unemployment insurance covered fishermen and seasonal workers, hospital insurance received financial support, and a system of equalization payments was worked out with the provinces.

In 1953 St Laurent led his party to an election victory. The country was run on a day-to-day basis by a small clique of federal civil servants, and increasingly the Liberals began to rely on Uncle Louis to win votes and remain in power. One claimed that they would keep running him 'stuffed' if necessary.

The Prime Minister had become a dedicated internationalist. He promoted world peace, turned the eyes of Canadians beyond the country's boundaries, backed the United Nations and helped to establish the North Atlantic Treaty Organization (NATO). When the North Koreans invaded South Korea in 1950, St Laurent sent Canadian troops to participate in the 'police action' organized by the United Nations. In 1954 he set off on a goodwill tour around the world, returning very fatigued. A diplomat who travelled with him recalled the Prime Minister's 'good sense and dignity' and his lack of pomposity. In New Delhi, before a formal dinner, St Laurent discovered that his trousers had been left on the plane, and a servant went out to buy a pair in a nearby bazaar. 'Mr St Laurent remained unperturbed and patient, with never a word of complaint,' the diplomat wrote of this incident. Two years later, in London, the same writer recorded that 'The Prime Minister seems sunk in melancholia.'

One day in 1956, Jack Pickersgill, Minister of Citizenship and Immigration, bumped into John Deutsch, Secretary of Treasury Board, while walking to work. They chatted about the recent deaths of two Canadian multimillionaires, Sir James Dunn and Izaak Walton Killam, whose estates had yielded $100 million in death duties. They agreed that the money should be used for something special, and Pickersgill suggested that half go to fund universities and the rest to endow a national arts council. The idea went up to St Laurent, who obtained the reluctant support of C D Howe, his Minister of Trade and

Commerce. The Prime Minister floated the concept in a speech to a university group in November, and introduced the bill himself to create the Canada Council. In doing so, he outlined his government's philosophy, stressing that it should 'support the cultural development of the nation, but not attempt to control it.' The Council came into being on 28 March 1957, by which time St Laurent's government was on its last legs.

In 1956 two crises erupted that wearied St Laurent. Just as Mackenzie King had relied upon him for support and advice, so St Laurent came increasingly to depend upon C D Howe to get things done. The dynamic, hard-driving, American-born engineer had organized the country's war effort and then presided over the postwar boom, serving as Minister of Trade and Commerce and also of Defence Production. Lacking any political sense, Howe viewed Canada as a huge corporation, the Cabinet as the Board of Directors and himself as its Chairman and Chief Executive Officer. In 1955 the 'Minister of Everything' acted in an overbearing manner during the debate on extending the mandate of his Department of Defence Production. When he tried to force a bill through Parliament in 1956 that would have provided $80 million to Trans-Canada Pipelines to help the company to link the gasfields of the West with the industrial East, he undid the government. The Opposition and other parties stalled the bill amid disorderly scenes in the House of Commons. The government invoked closure by calling for a vote to shut off debate on 1 June 1956, which became known as 'Black Friday.' St Laurent did little to ease the tensions in the House or the passage of the bill. Instead he sat reading a book while the arguments raged around him, like a fond father among his squabbling children.

The second crisis occurred in October 1956 when Israel, Britain and France invaded Egypt, and the Canadian government had to confront the realities of the new imperialism. Canada had sold planes to Egypt and anti-aircraft guns to Israel, but St Laurent strongly opposed the invasion. He claimed that the era of 'the supermen of Europe' had come to an end, and upset many Canadians who believed that Canada should support 'the old country,' right or wrong.

The time of Canada's innocence in international affairs had also come to an end. A weary diplomat wrote: 'Canadians ... are the family doctor whom no one has called in for consultation. We are the children of the midday who see all in the clear, shallow light.'

On 1 February 1957 the Liberals held a giant rally in Québec City to celebrate St Laurent's seventy-fifth birthday and to launch their election campaign. In the June election the Progressive Conservatives under John Diefenbaker gained seven seats more than the Liberals. St Laurent had no desire to hold on to power, and resigned as Prime Minister. Away from Ottawa, he sank into depression and then announced his retirement as Liberal leader.

When Parliament dissolved on 1 February 1958, St Laurent was not in Ottawa. Back home at last, his health improved and he took up the practice of law again. His wife died in 1966. The great gentleman who had been Canada's twelfth Prime Minister followed her seven years later, dying peacefully at the age of 91 on 25 July 1973.

Above: Work on Trans-Canada Pipeline, 1956.

Below: St Laurent at home in Québec City with two of his grandchildren, Marie (left) and Francine (right).

THE CHIEF

The Rt Hon

JOHN GEORGE DIEFENBAKER

21 June 1957 – 22 April 1963

*The right instincts were in him,
but throughout his stormy
stewardship, they languished in
the cupboard of his soul. He gave
the people a leadership cult
without leadership.*

PETER NEWMAN, *Renegade in Power* (1963)

Above: *John George Diefenbaker, at age seven, with his brother Elmer.*

I n the summer of 1957 a battle-scarred Volks-
wagen with a playpen on its roof crept timidly
up to the door of 24 Sussex Drive, the residence
of the Prime Minister in Ottawa. Here a uniformed
commissionaire saluted and told the couple in the
car that they must be lost. The woman said they had
come to visit her mom and dad. And who were they?
asked the commissionaire. 'Mr and Mrs Diefenbaker,' replied Carolyn Weir who tells the story in
her pictorial tribute to her stepfather. She recalls
that when Olive Diefenbaker greeted them, taking
her grandson in her arms, the commissionaire
saluted and stood to attention. He looked dazed and
was 'obviously thinking "if the Prime Minister of
Canada had a family who looks like this, what will
become of the country?"'

More than any other Canadian Prime Minister,
John George Diefenbaker raised conflicting emotions among Canadians. The tall, gangling figure, the
face trimmed with greying curls, the deepset eyes,
the histrionic gestures and the flamboyant language
were a boon to cartoonists, reporters and critics.
Duncan Macpherson of the *Toronto Star* drew
Diefenbaker as Marie Antoinette, Charles I, Nero, the
Cheshire Cat, Captain Ahab, the Red Queen and
Batman, and showed him walking on water in one
cartoon. Macpherson admitted that he 'had more fun
with Diefenbaker than anybody. . . . I had him going
as a wild man in my imagination and that's the way
he turned out.'

Diefenbaker, a man of large visions and petty
grudges, had a very different view of Canada and of
Canadians than any of his predecessors. A concerned and compassionate man, he had shared the
joys and sorrows of westerners through good times
and bad. Of southern German and Highland Scottish
stock, Diefenbaker claimed that he was 'the first
Prime Minister of this country of neither altogether
English nor French origin.' Born in September 1895
in Neustadt in Ontario's Grey County, Diefenbaker
did not reach the West until 1903. His teacher-father
moved first to Toronto and then to Fort Carlton in

the Northwest Territories, where he taught for three years before homesteading near Borden, Saskatchewan. The family arrived on its land with a cart, a cow, an organ, furniture and lots of books. In 1910 the family moved again so that the two sons could obtain a good education in Saskatoon.

The Canadian West opened up during John Diefenbaker's youth. Immigrants crowded in to start new lives. In that land of endless horizons, the daily round was dull, dreary and arduous. The attitude was that if you were not lucky today and in this place, perhaps tomorrow or another location would change your fortunes.

Young Diefenbaker immersed himself in books. One story tells of him looking up from a volume on Sir Wilfrid Laurier and telling the family that he was going to be premier of Canada some day. On the homestead he arose early to take grain to the elevators. He learned how harsh that new land could be when caught in a blizzard in March 1909 on his way back from a minstrel show with his uncle. The horse lost its way, and the pair spent the night huddled in the sledge and suffered frostbite. Diefenbaker's father became a government official in Saskatoon, and his two sons earned money selling newspapers. In 1910 John sold Prime Minister Laurier a paper, then sat and chatted with him. The boy recalled later, 'He told me something of his dreams for Canada and I told him my youthful ideas.' Then the paper boy told the Prime Minister that he 'couldn't waste any more time' on him – 'I must get about my work.'

At university Diefenbaker gained a reputation as a debater and a prankster. After graduating in 1915, he volunteered for service overseas and went to England with the Saskatoon Fusiliers in the following year. In London he saw and heard 'some of the giants of what were to be my twin loves, law and politics.' Diefenbaker would not talk about his military career; he was invalided home to Canada in 1917. He took his law degree at the University of Saskatoon, and then opened an office in Wakaw, a farming community 45 miles south of Prince Albert. Diefenbaker won his first murder case, built a flourishing practice and moved to Prince Albert in 1924.

Prince Albert lies on the so-called 'Prince Line' that links it with Prince George and Prince Rupert in British Columbia, marking the limit of economic agriculture. North of the line begins the Canadian subarctic, a land of vast, empty spaces and rich patches of natural resources. During his law career Diefenbaker saw a decade of prosperity on the Prairies followed by the miseries of the Depression. The people of the West teetered between optimism and the belief that things would get better, and the fear that they might get worse. Meanwhile, over the northern horizon, lay another 'tomorrow country' where people could strike it rich.

In Diefenbaker's days in law, the courts provided a form of theatrical entertainment for many rural dwellers where they could experience drama,

excitement, pathos, tragedy and humour – for free. Thus Diefenbaker had an ideal setting for his oratorical and histrionic talents. He would address each juror individually, chat with the person, appeal to his or her emotions and reasonableness. During one murder trial he grabbed his own throat and dropped to the floor to illustrate a point, outraging the judge.

Diefenbaker became a champion of the underdog, securing acquittals for individuals accused of murder and defending French Canadian school

Above: *A volunteer in the Saskatoon Fusiliers, Lt Diefenbaker went overseas in 1916. He is shown here (left) with two of his comrades, Lt Hugh Aird and Lt Allan Macmillan, who was killed in action.*

Left: *Leader of the Saskatchewan Conservative Association, Diefenbaker won a seat in the House of Commons in 1940.*

Above: *In the 1957 campaign for the Canadian Federal elections Diefenbaker's visionary concepts appealed to many Canadians.*

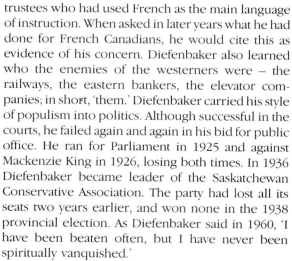

Right: *Diefenbaker celebrates his election victory with a characteristically histrionic gesture after a fishing excursion at Lac LaRonge in Saskatchewan.*

trustees who had used French as the main language of instruction. When asked in later years what he had done for French Canadians, he would cite this as evidence of his concern. Diefenbaker also learned who the enemies of the westerners were – the railways, the eastern bankers, the elevator companies; in short, 'them.' Diefenbaker carried his style of populism into politics. Although successful in the courts, he failed again and again in his bid for public office. He ran for Parliament in 1925 and against Mackenzie King in 1926, losing both times. In 1936 Diefenbaker became leader of the Saskatchewan Conservative Association. The party had lost all its seats two years earlier, and won none in the 1938 provincial election. As Diefenbaker said in 1960, 'I have been beaten often, but I have never been spiritually vanquished.'

His entry into federal politics came about through a strange incident, a piece of luck due to Diefenbaker being in the right place at the right time. Early in 1940 he was asked to give the keynote address at a federal nominating meeting in Imperial, north of Regina. He arrived to hear himself being nominated as a candidate, but withdrew in favour of a local man.

While preparing to leave, Diefenbaker spoke with a farmer who wanted some free legal advice. Then a friend rushed up and told him that the local candidate had withdrawn his name because he thought Diefenbaker had a better chance of winning the seat. The Conservatives won only 39 seats in the 1940 election, but John Diefenbaker took his and went to Ottawa.

He soon made his mark in the House of Commons, but found himself fighting on two fronts. A Prairie radical, Diefenbaker scared the Toronto moneymen who dominated the Conservative party and he baffled the Liberals who had never encountered anyone quite like this frontiersman from the edge of the wilderness. The new member supported the war effort and proved himself a dedicated monarchist. He also kept his eyes open for injustices, opposing the relocation of the Canadian Japanese in 1942, and increasingly casting himself in the role of the spokesman and defender of ordinary Canadians.

Political parties strive to catch and contain the energy of their dynamic members and channel it to support and promote their policies and programmes. John Diefenbaker, a loner, eventually captured his party and bent it to his will. He blocked the plans of the Conservatives to outlaw the Communist Party and championed Family Allowances in 1944, despite his party's opposition to them.

Diefenbaker's first wife, Edna, whom he had married in 1929, died of leukemia in 1951. Two years later he married Olive Freeman Palmer and was returned to Parliament again with the slogan 'Not a partisan cry, but a national need.' Diefenbaker consistently tried to show that he operated on his own political level, that he spoke for all Canadians. By 1953 the Liberals under Louis St Laurent had begun to show the strain of being too long in office. As their fortunes waned and as their arrogance showed, Diefenbaker, the outsider, began to look increasingly attractive as leader to his party and to many Canadians. This lone, articulate, dynamic individual spoke from his heart, and his words echoed in the minds of many Canadians. John Bracken and George Drew had followed Arthur Meighen as leaders of the Conservative party but neither had Diefenbaker's charisma. As a criminal lawyer, Diefenbaker had developed many skills that served him well in politics. He pointed his finger at the government, and urged the Opposition to turn out the Liberals.

In 1956 Diefenbaker's persistence finally paid off, and he won the leadership of the Progressive Conservatives on the first ballot. A one-man political party, the new leader closed in on the ailing, failing government, and the Conservatives won seven seats more than the Liberals in the 1957 election.

Lester Pearson, the new Liberal leader, then made a monumental error by suggesting that Diefenbaker resign and hand the government to him. Diefenbaker poured out his scorn and contempt, using a secret government document to show that the

Liberals had painted a false picture of the economy before and during the election. Then he dissolved Parliament and set off on the campaign trail. Allister Grosart, a public relations man, packaged Diefenbaker for public consumption, even composing a song to emphasize the correct pronunciation of 'Diefenbay-ker's' name. The Prime Minister used television and the campaign platform to great advantage in the 1958 election. Diefenbaker had a curious way with words, which seemed to curve back on themselves as they were spoken. He once claimed that his course 'was determined' for him as a youngster, 'undeviating and unchanging.' Then he added that 'It was all determined for me. I determined myself that was the thing I was going to do – and I determined it because of my mixed racial origins.' The mystical aspects of Diefenbaker's nature appealed to many Canadians tired of the Liberal's bland, businesslike, managerial style of operation. The Prime Minister saw 'a nation of 50 million' and in Winnipeg spoke of 'one Canada . . . where Canadians will have preserved to them the control of their own economic and political life.' Just

Above: *Lester B Pearson (right), the new Liberal leader in 1958, shown chatting jovially with newly elected Prime Minister Diefenbaker (centre). Actually, the two were highly disputatious over the outcome of the elections.*

Left: John G Diefenbaker and his Cabinet in July 1958.

Lower left: Queen Elizabeth II with Prince Philip opens Canada's Parliament October 14, 1957.

Below: 'Dief the Chief' fraternizes with an Indian constituent at Duck Lake, Saskatchewan, in June 1953. As Prime Minister he appointed the first Indian senator.

dians, especially those living on the margins of society. He arranged sales of wheat to China to boost farmers' incomes, passed the Agricultural Rehabilitation and Development Act to eliminate rural poverty, subsidized the Maritimes, developed a National Oil Policy and gave Indians the vote.

In 1960 Diefenbaker brought in what he considered his most significant achievement – the Canadian Bill of Rights. He also led the movement to expel South Africa from the Commonwealth in the following year. During his tenure General Georges Vanier, a distinguished French Canadian soldier, was named Governor-General, simultaneous translation made the House of Commons bilingual and the government began to issue cheques in both languages. 'Roads to Resources' opened up the North, and the National Productivity Council set about improving the competitiveness of Canadian industry. Alas, the roads into the North often led into barren wildernesses, and Diefenbaker failed to grasp that urbanization represented a bigger challenge to his government than opening up the northern frontier did. He knew as little about that region as Macdonald did about the West.

Many of the government's problems lay beyond its control. Western Europe and Japan, recovered from the war, became competitive again in world markets. The programmes of social justice proved to be costly and needed large numbers of civil servants to run them. Diefenbaker started to believe that his

as his idol, Sir John A Macdonald, had thrown open the West, so Diefenbaker turned the eyes of Canadians northwards where he saw 'a new Canada – a Canada of the North!'

The Conservatives won 208 seats in the 1958 landslide. The prophet had led his people out of the wilderness and into power. Magnificent in opposition, a great campaigner who could sway multitudes, Diefenbaker in office showed that mystics don't make good managers.

The problems created by the Prime Minister's highly personal style of leadership were compounded by poor economic conditions. The Conservative party, out of power for more than 20 years, simply did not have experienced people who knew how to run the country. 'Dief the Chief,' as he became known, had great difficulty making decisions, so he tended to postpone them. Espousing the idea of social justice as his guide, Diefenbaker had no firm policies or concepts to give direction to his government, nor could he manage men well. He did not bother to find the Québec anchor so vital to the stability of the Canadian ship of state. Léon Balcer, a potential candidate for the role, had opposed Diefenbaker's efforts to become party leader. He was therefore relegated to the unimportant position of Solicitor-General, because the Chief divided people into friends and enemies, and never forgave anyone he believed to have opposed his will.

Yet the Prime Minister brought to Ottawa a new understanding of the West and of ordinary Cana-

Above: *At the Wallacetown Fair in Ontario in 1960 Diefenbaker fills his chosen role as spokesman and defender of ordinary Canadians.*

civil servants were against him as his grandiose schemes began to fall apart. Unemployment rose and the government increasingly relied on budget deficits to finance its operations. In 1959 the government scrapped the development of the CF-105 Arrow supersonic fighter after spending $780 million on it. The Conservatives hoped to rely on American Bomarc missiles to defend the country. Every single plane was reduced to scrap as if to wipe the memory of the Arrow from the minds of Canadians, and 13,800 highly skilled Canadians lost their jobs.

James Coyne, governor of the Bank of Canada, became convinced that the country was on the road to ruin. He publicly preached the gospel of restraint. Instead of curbing Coyne, the government allowed him to ramble on, then suddenly fired him in 1961 and gave the Liberals a handy martyr.

In 1962 Minister of Finance Donald Fleming introduced a budget that proposed a deficit of $745 million. Despite a government austerity programme, investors deserted the Canadian dollar, and to avert a foreign exchange crisis the government devalued it to 92.5 cents American.

In the international sphere Canadians became acutely aware that their country lay between two nuclear superpowers that distrusted each other. Diefenbaker liked President Dwight Eisenhower, but viewed President John F Kennedy as an arrogant young man and an enemy. Kennedy saw the Prime Minister as a mischief-making old man who could not be trusted. When the American president confronted the Russians in October 1962 and told them to remove their missiles from Cuba or face nuclear war, Diefenbaker dithered before coming out in support of Kennedy's stance.

Then came Canada's own missile crisis. The government had agreed to accept two Bomarc missile bases on Canadian soil. To be effective the missiles, which had a limited range, had to carry nuclear warheads. Douglas Harkness, Minister of Defence, wanted the missiles armed. Howard Green, Minister for External Affairs, had pushed strongly for disarmament at the United Nations and opposed the installation of nuclear missiles. Diefenbaker tried to get the best of both worlds by agreeing that the Bomarcs would be armed with nuclear warheads only in an emergency. Then a

Above: *Cartoonists found Diefenbaker a ready target.*

Left: *Young people of varying ethnic backgrounds regarded Diefenbaker as a friend.*

Below: *Diefenbaker with his wife in the Prime Minister's official residence in Ottawa.*

retiring Supreme Commander of NATO, on a visit to Ottawa in January 1963, let slip the fact that Canada had accepted nuclear weapons for its forces in Europe.

Relations between Canada and the United States sank to a new low. Diefenbaker vowed that he would never accept 'external domination,' nor would he accept internal direction from his own party. In the 1962 election the Conservatives had won 116 seats to the 99 held by the Liberals, and operated a minority government. On 3 February 1963 a group of Cabinet ministers confronted Diefenbaker, and Douglas Harkness told him that they had lost their confidence in him. He had the courage to resign, but the rest of the Cabinet backed down under the Prime Minister's fierce glare.

Diefenbaker did not change his way. He became convinced that his enemies were out to destroy him. 'No leader can go forward when he has to turn around to see who is trying to trip him up from behind,' he intoned. On 4 February 1963 Lester Pearson moved 'that this government, because of lack of leadership, the breakdown of unity in the Cabinet, and confusion and indecision in dealing with national and international problems does not have the confidence of the Canadian people.' The three opposition parties voted for the motion on the following day, and Diefenbaker's government fell.

Right: *The installation of nuclear warheads on missiles, supported by Defence Minister Harkness, proved a test for Diefenbaker, whose External Affairs Minister had backed disarmament at the United Nations.*

Below: *In an effort to bolster flagging relations with the United States, Diefenbaker visited President Kennedy in Washington in 1963. They are shown here in the Oval Office at the White House.*

The 1963 election campaign focused on Diefenbaker. He claimed that everyone was against him, 'except the people.' He repeated this theme many times, stating that 'there are great forces against me, great interests against me, both national and international.' At a meeting towards the end of the campaign, he claimed: 'I ask myself, is a thing right, and if it is right I do it.'

After losing the election the Chief stayed on as party leader, while his party made strenuous efforts to remove him. In 1967, with opinion polls showing the Conservatives with 25 percent of the popular vote, lower even than the New Democratic Party (NDP), 'they' finally got Diefenbaker. He waited until the last minute to declare his candidacy at the leadership convention, and came fifth on the first ballot. It must have confirmed in his mind that there were more of 'them' out there than he imagined. Robert Stanfield, a wealthy, low-key lawyer from a Nova Scotia textile family, became the new Conservative Prime Minister. This mild, highly intelligent man provided a striking contrast to the Chief.

Diefenbaker retained his seat in the House of Commons – and his wit. He claimed in 1975 that he was disturbed 'because my doctors tell me I'm as sound as a dollar.' He also noted, 'I have lived history. I've made history and I know I'll have my place in history.' Just to make sure of that place he wrote his memoirs, *One Canada*. Diefenbaker became testier and more demanding as he aged. A Macpherson cartoon showed him as a shawled pensioner with a needlepoint Union Jack in his lap. The voters sent him back to Parliament in May 1979. On 15 August he tried out the new snooker table in the Press Club, and on the following morning he passed away peacefully in his office, a 'House of Commons man' to the end.

Even in death Diefenbaker kept the eye of the public on him. He arranged his own funeral, and as the train carrying his coffin crossed the country, many Canadians gave this remarkable man a last farewell. On 22 August he was buried with his beloved wife Olive, who had died in 1976, near the Honourable John G Diefenbaker Centre at the University of Saskatoon. In September 1986 John Diefenbaker returned to Parliament Hill when his statue joined those of Sir John A Macdonald and other past Prime Ministers. The Chief's statue stands close to that of Queen Victoria. He would have liked that.

Top right: *Diefenbaker's often repeated claim that 'there are great interests against me' proved true in the 1963 election campaign.*

Right: *As an orator Diefenbaker tended to be flamboyant and theatrical.*

'MIKE'

The Rt Hon
LESTER BOWLES
PEARSON

22 April 1963 – 20 April 1968

His mind . . . had never revealed its inner contents to any colleague, perhaps not even to its owner. Usually considered a genial extrovert, Pearson was the most popular and the most solitary person of his time.

BRUCE HUTCHINSON, *Mr. Prime Minister* (1964)

On 2 April 1965 Prime Minister Lester Pearson spoke at Temple University in Philadelphia, Pennsylvania, advocating a pause in the American bombing of Vietnam. Afterwards President Lyndon Johnson summoned him to Camp David, the presidential retreat in Maryland, and Pearson asked him what he thought of his speech. 'Awful,' replied the President, and took the Prime Minister out on the terrace. Charles Ritchie, Canadian Ambassador to the United States, watched in horror as the President verbally assaulted the Prime Minister. The President even grabbed Pearson's coat lapels to make his points more forcibly. The Prime Minister, Ritchie explained to a presidential aide, had spoken at Temple University as 'a Nobel Prize lecturer at an academic occasion,' not as a politician.

Pearson continually had the problem of seeing himself above politics. The Liberal party had seized upon him as their leader because of his international reputation. A journalist wrote of Pearson during the 1958 election campaign that he seemed 'less concerned with voting ... than with the triumph of sound principles of government.'

Born in April 1897 in Newtonbrook, now part of Toronto, Lester Bowles Pearson grew up in southern Ontario as his Methodist minister father moved around different parishes. Genteel poverty, Methodist piety and a belief in progress marked his youth. He later claimed that his motto was 'Not to seek success but to deserve it.' Pearson always did the best in any job he held. He had no burning ambition, but a great deal of intelligence and good sense, moving crablike through life rather than straight ahead.

After graduating from high school in Hamilton, young Lester went to Victoria College at the University of Toronto. In 1915, studying a Latin poet in the library, he decided, 'war can't be this bad' and enlisted as No 1059 Private Pearson, Canadian Army Medical Corps. He arrived in London on his eighteenth birthday, afire with heroic visions of battle derived from English boys' stories. He ended up on one of the forgotten fronts of the First World War, serving through winter mud and summer heat in a field hospital at Salonika, Greece. He pulled a few strings to secure a commission in the Royal Flying Corps, but instead he ended up in Oxford, England, training as an infantry officer. Next he was sent to join the Royal Flying Corps and crashed his plane, sustaining some scratches and bruises. 'Restless and eager for diversion,' as he put it, Pearson set off for a night on the town in London. On the way back to camp a bus hit him, and he returned to Canada as a flying instructor. Had he become an infantry officer or a fighter pilot, however, his life expectancy in France would have been measured in weeks. The squadron leader during his flight training decided that Lester was 'no name for a fighter pilot,' and christened him 'Mike,' a name that stuck.

Pearson returned to Victoria College, completed a degree in history, then articled with a lawyer, and

spent a few months stuffing sausages and clerking in Chicago. Then he decided on an academic career, won a fellowship to Oxford and studied history there. He also played hockey, lacrosse, rugger and tennis, developing an interest in sport that lasted all his life. When Pearson returned to lecture at the University of Toronto in 1923, he also coached the

Above: Pearson *as pilot in First World War.*
Far left: *The Reverend and Mrs E A Pearson with family. Lester is standing on chair.*
Below: *As First Secretary at the Canadian High Commission in London in 1936.*

Massey, dean of Pearson's college, noted that there was 'something curiously loose-jointed and sloppy about his make-up. . . .' Perhaps it was these very qualities that Canadian diplomacy needed when Pearson joined External Affairs. An able writer, Pearson had a knack for negotiating, preparing briefs and papers, attending conferences and searching for common ground on international issues.

When the Bennett government came to power in 1930, Pearson's abilities caught the eye of the Prime Minister. He served as Secretary to the Royal Commission on Price Spreads, and handled press and information matters at the Imperial Preference Conference in 1932. Gaining a name for hard work,

university hockey team. Two years later he married Maryon Elspeth Moody, one of his students.

As Canada established more control over its own foreign affairs, those serving Prime Minister Mackenzie King looked around for talent to staff the growing diplomatic service. Pearson wrote the exams, came first and started a new career at age 32. Even in 1928 Canada had only a dozen officers in its External Affairs office in Ottawa and missions in Washington, London, Paris and Tokyo. Vincent

Above: *Meeting with John Foster Dulles (right) in Washington, DC, on trade in 1954.*

Right: *Pearson at UN 1957.*

Below: *Canadian UNEF contingent parading in Rafah, Egypt, August 29, 1958.*

humour and tact, Pearson went to London three years later as First Secretary at the Canadian High Commission. Watching the rise of Hitler, he warned Mackenzie King of the coming of war. The Prime Minister once wrote that when Pearson came into his office, he was struck by 'his fine face and appearance. There was a light which shone through his countenance.' But he paid no heed to Pearson's warnings about Hitler's ambitions. When war broke out and Westminster Hall was bombed, King asked Pearson to secure some stones from it to incorporate into his folly at Kingsmere.

Pearson returned to Ottawa in 1941, then went to Canada's Washington DC embassy. The friendly, sports-loving diplomat became popular with the press and soon knew everybody who was anybody in the American capital. The Canadian Minister to Washington said he didn't mind Mike 'running the whole legation but I wish, sometimes, that he'd tell me what we're doing.' In 1944 Pearson became Canada's Ambassador to the United States, and two years later Undersecretary of State for External Affairs.

While driving around the Bois de Boulogne in Paris in a horse-drawn carriage with Pearson in 1945, Mackenzie King suggested that his companion was 'cut out for politics.' Pearson disagreed then, but soon after Louis St Laurent became Prime Minister in 1948 he invited Pearson to join the Cabinet as Minister for External Affairs. With Germany, France and Italy in ruins, Britain and France exhausted, and the Soviet Union and the United States increasingly distrustful of each other, Canada had a chance to play a mediating role in the world and to wage peace. Mike Pearson's affable, unstuffy style helped this process immensely. With a smile as fixed as his bow tie, Mike played the role of enabler in international affairs. With typical Canadian modesty, Pearson did not promote himself and obscured his feelings with a sardonic wit. He hated personal unpleasantness, and did all he could to avoid it.

Pearson bent his abilities to strengthening the United Nations, but also assisted in creating the North Atlantic Treaty Organization to defend the West. When war broke out in Korea in 1950 Canada provided troops for the United Nations army to defend South Korea after the North Korean invasion. Pearson served as President of the United Nations Assembly in 1952, and paid a friendly visit to the Soviet Union in 1955 where he experienced 'conviviality beyond the line of duty.'

The end of innocence for Canada came in 1956, when Britain, France and Israel invaded Egypt over the plans of its ruler, Colonel Gamal Nasser, to take over the Suez Canal. It was as if 'a beloved uncle had been accused of rape,' as a British magazine put it. Pearson worked frantically to establish the United Nations peacekeeping force. It separated the warring states, the invaders moved out and faces were saved. In the House of Commons, however, Pearson was accused of 'knifing Canada's best friends in the back,' but his actions earned him the Nobel Prize for Peace in 1957. Pearson's reaction to hearing of the award was typical – 'Gosh!'

The Liberals, turned out of office in 1957, made Pearson their leader in the next year. He had little feel for politics, and earned Diefenbaker's contempt with his ill-fated attempt to recover the government. During the 1958 election Pearson's shortcomings as a politician began to show. He lacked Diefenbaker's courtroom tricks, sense of righteousness and command of rhetoric. Instead he tended to lecture his audiences. The Liberals campaigned on the slogan 'Peace, Prosperity, Pearson,' but were reduced to 49 seats. Pearson developed a hatred of Diefenbaker, whom he believed to be ruining the country, and he set about rebuilding the Liberal party. A conference at Kingston in 1960 allowed a younger generation of Liberals to express their discontent with traditional policies and to hear new ideas on the best way to run Canada. As he found his feet as a politician, Pearson

Below: *In 1957 Lester B Pearson was awarded the Nobel Peace Prize for his work on behalf of the UN in resolving the 1956 Arab-Israeli war. He is seen here in Oslo beside the bust of Alfred Nobel.*

Left: *Pearson acknowledging his election as leader of the Liberal Party January 1958.*

Below left: *A critical view of Pearson's 'man of the Centre' stance.*

supported the thrust towards 'small-l Liberalism.' A Liberal, he claimed, 'is a man of the Centre, moving forward. But while we are in the middle of the road, we don't stand still.' Thus did Pearson's concept of Canada as a 'middle power' find expression in domestic politics. The Liberal leader also improved his platform style, delivering a long address in Vancouver while demonstrators pelted him with peas. In January 1963 Pearson came out in favour of nuclear weapons for Canada, and Pierre Elliot Trudeau called him 'the unfrocked pope of peace.'

In the April election of that year, the Prairies voted Conservative, the cities went Liberal and Pearson came to power in a minority government. As Prime Minister, Pearson promised 'Sixty Days of Decision,' but the new government got off to a bad start. Its first major piece of legislation, the budget, caused Pearson's government trouble at home and abroad. In preparing it, Minister of Finance Walter Gordon brought in three Toronto consultants, ignoring the advice of his own staff. Gordon, an ardent nationalist, proposed a takeover tax on foreign acquisitions of Canadian companies, a measure aimed clearly at the Americans. Canadian business people attacked the budget, and the use of consultants scandalized the Opposition. Initially, relations with President Kennedy had been cordial, but the honeymoon with the United States ended with Gordon's budget. The Minister of Finance was eventually forced to withdraw the takeover tax.

Left: *Prime Minister Pearson (left) with President Kennedy during a visit to Washington in 1963.*

Below: *George Vanier, Canada's Governor-General, speaking at the New Maple Leaf Flag ceremony in Ottawa on 15 February 1965 when Canada finally received its own flag.*

Top left: *Finance Minister Walter Gordon, an ardent nationalist, caused Pearson's government trouble at home and abroad when he proposed a takeover tax on foreign acquisitions of Canadian companies.*

Above: *In 1966 Pearson had to intervene personally in a longshoremen's strike.*

Right: *General Charles de Gaulle, president of France, arriving in Québec 23 July 1967 for a five-day tour of Canada.*

Canada had begun to benefit from the austerity measures of the Conservatives by the time the Liberals came to power, and the economy began to expand. In 1963 unemployment stood at 5.5 percent and two years later it dropped to a low of 3.6 percent. In 1966 the Prime Minister intervened personally in a strike of longshoremen at the St Lawrence ports and of workers on the seaway. Fearing that shipments of wheat to the Soviet Union would be disrupted and the completion of Expo '67 delayed, he authorized contracts providing an increase of 15 percent a year to settle the strike. Union leaders in all sectors of society, especially those in government-owned and operated bodies, began to press for the 'Pearson formula' in all wage settlements.

With the populations in the cities increasing and expectations rising, provincial premiers found their social and educational budgets under pressure. The federal government tried to work with the provinces to develop a universal pension plan, but Premier Lesage of Québec informed Pearson that he would develop his own scheme. Increasingly the Québécois wanted to run their own affairs, to be *maître chez nous*.

In his election campaign, Pearson had promised the traditional remedy for tensions in Canada – a royal commission – to address the problems of separatism and relations between English and French Canadians. The Royal Commission on Bilingualism and Biculturalism reported that Canada might come apart. As Québec separatism bloomed, the federal government initiated some symbolic gestures to keep the country together and to strengthen the feelings of national unity. Canada finally received its own flag, Trans-Canada Airlines became Air Canada and Minister of Defence Paul Hellyer unified the Canadian Armed Forces. Canadians flocked to Montreal to see Expo '67 while across the country communities celebrated the one hundredth anniversary of Confederation. President Charles de Gaulle of France, however, rained on the parade. While on an official visit to Canada, he shouted *Vive le Québec Libre!* in Montreal. Pearson rebuked him and de Gaulle left the country in a huff.

Pearson's government established a Department of Regional Economic Expansion, expanded the welfare state and initiated programmes aimed at eliminating poverty and regional disparity. Diefenbaker had aroused the awareness of Canadians about the disadvantaged in the country, and the Liberals set out to do good works among them. Many of their programmes, however, were poor imitations of those launched during the American War of Poverty. Pearson hoped to channel the energy of Canada's youth into socially useful outlets by setting up a domestic version of the American Peace Corps. One source claimed that the Prime Minister wanted the Company of Young Canadians to clean statues and monuments. Instead it became a refuge for rebels without a cause, young people at a loose end and radicals bent on fighting the system with

government money.

Pearson decided to step down as leader of the Liberals during the centennial year. In an address he claimed that his failures had been due to his reliance 'entirely on the Sermon on the Mount as the guideline for Cabinet solidarity.'

In retirement Pearson chaired a study for the World Bank, which issued a report entitled *Partners in Development* in October 1969. He taught at Ottawa's Carleton University, received the Order of Merit and became Chairman of the Montreal Expos. He also began to write his memoirs, entitled simply *Mike*, at which point he learned he had cancer, and worked frantically to complete the book. Courageous to the end and a much-loved man in Canada, 'Mike' died on 27 December 1972, and was buried in a small cemetery in the Gatineau Hills during a blizzard on the last day of the year.

Above: *Pearson at bat in a parliamentary ball game.*

Left: *Crowds waving French flags and banners proclaiming 'liberté' for Québec, jam around President de Gaulle's car after his visit to Québec's City Hall.*

THE PHILOSOPHER KING

The Rt Hon
PIERRE ELLIOTT TRUDEAU

20 April 1968 – 4 June 1979

3 March 1980 – 30 June 1984

> *His outstanding character personifies the striking contrast of this nation. He is warm. He is cold. He is wild. He is serene. But, above all, he is honest with himself and others.*
>
> DONALD JOHNSTON, *Up The Hill* (1986)

Below: *The site of Expo '67, the gigantic World's Fair that was held in Montreal in 1967.*

Right: *Prime Minister Trudeau.*

In 1969 Prime Minister Trudeau visited Tukto-yaktuk at the mouth of the Mackenzie River in the Northwest Territories and chatted for an hour with Eddie Gruben. The Inuit, a former trapper and hunter, had a Grade 3 education and ran a taxi and hauling business. Trudeau suggested that the Inuit become involved in offshore oil and gas development in the nearby Beaufort Sea. As Gruben put it: 'I took his advice and when the time came, I was ready with the equipment they needed.' He became Canada's first Inuit millionaire. W A Wilson, a respected journalist, accompanied Trudeau on another trip to the Arctic in 1970. Those with whom he travelled, he wrote, found in Trudeau 'a sensitive, sympathetic observer who approaches the people and the things he is seeing with a highly intelligent mind.' Trudeau was the first Canadian Prime Minister to visit the Arctic and talk with the people there.

In the early days of his government, Trudeau seemed to hold the promise of creating a new type of administration, intelligent and compassionate, one that would usher in an era of justice, freedom and opportunities for all. By the time the Prime Minister left office in 1984, the Liberal party lay in a shambles and Canadians wondered what had gone wrong under a philosopher-king who could quote Plato and shoot rapids in a canoe with equal dexterity.

The country's one-hundredth birthday celebrations in 1967 and the success of Expo '67 generated a great sense of euphoria among Canadians, heightening feelings of nationalism. The rising middle class needed a leader who would personify all the best qualities of the country. The quest for a charismatic leader who could bring a nation into the modern world through the sheer force of his personality was characteristic of new nations throughout the developing world in the postwar era. Pierre Elliott Trudeau met the Canadian need for a new type of leader as the country entered a turbulent time. By any standard, he was a remarkable individual.

Born in Montréal on 18 October 1919, Joseph Pierre Yves Elliott Trudeau came from a wealthy and cultured family and grew up bilingual. Charlie, his

Right: *Maurice Duplessis, premier of Québec for twenty-three years, ran the province as though it were a fiefdom.*

Next right: *René Lévesque, founder and head of the separatist Parti Québécois.*

Far right: *President Julius Nyerere of Tanzania held discussions in Canada in August 1977 prior to visiting US.*

Far right, below: *This Macpherson cartoon of 12 September 1968 reflects the view of many Canadians when Trudeau became Prime Minister.*

Below: *Called 'The Three Wise Men,' Jean Marchand (left) and Gérard Pelletier (right) were, with Trudeau (center), among the young intellectuals who joined forces in seeking reform in Québec.*

father, a lawyer and businessman, developed a chain of gas stations and built the family fortune through shrewd investments. His mother, Grace, a small delicate woman of Scottish descent, visited museums, attended concerts and befriended artists. As Trudeau put it, 'My father taught me order and discipline, and my mother freedom and fantasy.'

During the Depression the family did not suffer. Pierre went to school in a chauffeur-driven limousine. At the exclusive Jesuit run Brébeuf College, he developed and disciplined his mind and his body. He also became a loner, opposing the stream of nationalistic thought that had began to trickle through Québec. During World War II he opposed conscription, and studied law at the Université de Montréal. Called to the bar in 1944, Trudeau articled briefly with a law firm, then drifted back into academic life, studying politics and economics at Harvard, the Sorbonne in Paris and the London School of Economics. Afterwards he went vagabonding across Europe and Asia, flirting with danger. He was arrested in Palestine and crossed the India-Pakistan border, and he later engaged in adolescent pranks like hurling snowballs at Stalin's statue in Moscow. On another occasion he tried to reach Cuba by canoe from Florida.

Returning to Canada from his world travels in 1949, Trudeau sought outlets for his restless, reckless, romantic idealism. Under Maurice Duplessis, Premier of Québec from 1936 to 1939 and from 1949 to 1959, the province remained conservative, corrupt and clerically dominated. 'Le Chef' modernized the economy but refused to reform the instruments of government. Promoting his own brand of defensive nationalism, Duplessis fought any attempts by the federal government to extend its power, even refusing grants for universities.

Like many young university-trained intellectuals, Trudeau burned with a desire for change and social justice, but he lacked an understanding of the ways in which to make Québec into a new society. In 1949 asbestos workers in the Eastern Townships went on strike, and the government moved to crush them. Here Trudeau received his education in the uses of government power. With his friend Gérard Pelletier, he supported the strikers and came to know Jean Marchand, the top labour leader. The three later entered federal politics together and became known as 'The Three Wise Men.'

In 1950 Trudeau went to Ottawa as an economic advisor in the Privy Council Office to learn what happened in the corridors of power in the capital. He also helped to found a magazine called *Cité Libre* to rally the foes of Duplessis. Trudeau wrote many of the articles for the publication, advocating democracy for Québec, hammering the federal Liberals and opposing nationalism. As Pelletier wrote in his autobiography, *Years of Impatience: 1950-1960*, the

ginger group of young intellectuals saw 'a Québec and a Canada invisible on their surface' with 'hidden currents of rare power' beginning to move people. As 'the winds of the world' blew through the old structures of Québec, they mingled with 'the breeze of separatism.' The radicals did not have a unified agenda for change. René Lévesque, later Premier of a separatist Québec, belonged to the reformers. In 1956 Trudeau helped to found a left-wing movement called the Rassemblement, but it fell apart two years later because of squabbling among the leaders.

In 1959 Premier Duplessis died. Jean Lesage and the Liberals came to power, pledged to bring Québec into the modern world. The new premier began to talk about a familiar theme, that the people of the province should be masters in their own house. He also spoke about 'the hour of the last chance' for Confederation. In 1963 terrorist bombs destroyed mail boxes in Montreal as separatists struck at the symbols of federal power. Trudeau attacked separatism in *Cité Libre*. Even in 1964 a French Canadian professor, while describing Trudeau as 'easily the most talented intellectual in Québec' claimed that he had 'frittered away his gifts in aimless intellectual nonconformity and bohemian pleasures.'

A year later Pierre Elliott Trudeau stood for the federal Liberals in Mount Royal, a part of Montréal laid out in the shape of a Union Jack, and he won the seat. With Jean Marchand and Gérard Pelletier, Trudeau went to Ottawa to help Pearson's Liberals understand what was happening in Québec. Trudeau became Pearson's Parliamentary Secretary and then Minister of Justice in May 1967. His habit of wearing sandals and an ascot in the House of Commons enraged John Diefenbaker, but he set to work with a will to modernize Canada's Criminal Code. He showed a talent for coining aphorisms, claiming that 'The state has no place in the nation's bedrooms' as he liberalized the laws on divorce, abortion and homosexuality. When a television interviewer asked Trudeau in March 1967 if he wanted to become Prime Minister, he replied, 'Not very badly.' Then he quoted Plato: 'Men who want very badly to head the country shouldn't be trusted.' At the Dominion-Provincial conference in February 1968, Trudeau captured a great deal of media and public attention. He had an impressive television persona, debated well and gave the impression of strength and depth in his presentations. He had the look of a new kind of politician.

Persuaded by friends to run for the Liberal leadership, Trudeau won it at the convention in Ottawa in April 1968. He dissolved Parliament and urged Canadians to elect a majority Liberal government. On 23 June he had his wish and the Liberals had their mandate.

Photographs from the early days of Trudeaumania show the Prime Minister clearly enjoying himself. Here was a man for all seasons who went among the people and made personal contact with them, an intellectual with a broad smile, a rose in his lapel and a friendly open manner. Trudeau had a costume for every occasion – a slouch hat and Dracula cape for a Grey Cup football game; cowboy clothes for the Calgary Stampede; and a black tie, tuxedo and a flower in his lapel to take Barbra Streisand to the National Arts Centre. He also had a face for every audience – smiling, quizzical, mocking, serene, the almond-shaped eyes and the planes of the cheeks giving the face an enigmatic cast.

The new government set out its intent in the Speech from the Throne, claiming that 'the attainment of a just society is the cherished hope of civilized men.' Trudeau had said in an interview that this society 'is the kind of society freedom would establish,' but in his enigmatic way, he did not spell out the ways and instruments that would bring about the 'Just Society.' The Throne Speech also promised to ameliorate regional disparities. Parliament, he noted, was too far removed 'from the people it serves; its operations . . . too slow and ponderous; its deliberations . . . often insufficiently informed; and its decisions . . . too few and much delayed.' Few Canadians would have quibbled with this diagnosis, and the Liberal government introduced 'Participatory Democracy' to remedy these ills. The term sounded good on paper, but proved difficult to

put into practise. The Throne Speech also promised advancement for Francophones in the public service. If their aspirations could be met in the federal government, they might be less interested in working to create a separate state in Québec.

The government's style of operation, however, relied heavily on two of Trudeau's concepts. He believed in 'reason over passion' and in creating 'counterweights.' Government programmes would be rationalized, and no individual or group allowed too much power over Canada's destiny. In Parliament, Trudeau showed an abrasive lack of tact in dealing with members. When they were 'fifty yards from Parliament, they are no longer honourable members, they are just nobodies,' he jeered. Trudeau also showed his arrogance in dealing with other Canadians. At a Liberal rally in Manitoba in December 1968, he responded to a question by asking, 'Well, why should I sell the Canadian farmers' wheat?'

The government launched an array of new programmes to serve a wide range of interest groups. Opportunities for Youth, New Horizons for seniors and the Local Initiative Programme for the unemployed provided government money to keep people busy and happy. Pressure groups concerned about the environment and other problems received federal funds to harass federal agencies. Sports groups were subsidized. As the 'outsiders' in Canadian society began to benefit from government grants, the middle class – the traditional power base of the Liberal party – felt betrayed and forgotten.

Above: A parody of Trudeau's unconventional lifestyle.

Top right: Trudeau promotes his vision of 'The Just Society' to a group in Ottawa 17 July 1971.

Right: Under Trudeau the government subsidized sports with stunning results. Canada's Steve Podborski became the first North American to win the Men's World Cup downhill ski championship in 1982, and at the Winter Olympics in Montreal in 1984, among other achievements by Canadians, Kathy Kreiner won the Women's Giant Slalom in unsurpassed record time.

Far right: President Richard Nixon (seated left) during his 1972 visit to Ottawa. Trudeau is at podium.

Above: *In the 1976 provincial election Lévesque's separatist Parti Québécois triumphed over Trudeau's Liberal party, owing in part to Trudeau's severe measures against separatist terrorists during the October kidnapping crisis.*

Right: *Margaret Sinclair, whom Trudeau married in 1971. Her outspokenness attracted considerable media attention.*

Government policies and programmes favoured the constituency of the NDP, the casualties of social change for whom that party claimed to speak. The bureaucrats sought the answer to the problems of change in the minds of American academics rather than in the hearts of Canadians or in the experiences of those skilled in handling social tensions. The bureaucracy expanded as university-trained specialists staffed the new programmes.

In the fall of 1970, separatist terrorists kidnapped Pierre Laporte, the Québec Minister of Labour, and James Cross, the British Trade Commissioner, in Montréal. Québec Premier Bourassa panicked, and Trudeau promulgated the War Measures Act at 4 am on 15 October 1970 to 'apprehend an insurrection.' His action horrified those concerned with civil liberties, but most Canadians approved of it. Aislin, the Montréal cartoonist, drew Jean Marchand clutching the phone books of cities in Québec and saying, 'We now have a list of FLQ suspects.' The *Front de Libération du Québec* (FLQ) made a series of ransom demands, killed Laporte, but let Cross go free. Rather than being a large conspiracy poised to take over the country, the FLQ proved to be made up of two groups of rather pathetic social misfits using nationalism as a cover for terrorist activities. The October crisis paved the way for the victory of Réne Lévesque and the Parti Québécois in the provincial election of 1976.

Trudeau married Margaret Sinclair in 1971. Much younger than her husband, this flower child campaigned with the Prime Minister during the 1972 election, telling Canadians how much he had taught her about love. Under their new leader, Robert Stanfield, the Conservatives won 107 seats, two fewer than the Liberals. Trudeau became depressed. His minority government developed a new national energy policy, reformed the social security and tax systems and set up the Foreign Investment Review Agency. Justice Thomas Berger examined the impact of the proposed Mackenzie Valley Pipeline in great detail. By appealing to nationalist and environmental interests, the Liberals reassured Canadians of their good intentions and secured a majority in the election of July 1974.

Then things began to fall apart. Trudeau and his wife separated in the spring of 1977 and divorced in 1984. The rise in oil prices compounded problems of recession, inflation, regional disparity and unemployment in the early 1980s. The Prime Minister increasingly concentrated power in his own hands; at Cabinet meetings the ministers felt like students at

a university seminar being questioned by a professor. With a separatist government in power in Québec after 1976, Trudeau's already strained relations with the provinces became worse. He persisted in using a confrontational style with the premiers, who distrusted his centralist tendencies. The western provinces claimed that they were losing billions of dollars in revenue because of the Liberals' 'made in Canada' oil-pricing system.

The Liberals had mocked Stanfield's election promise of mandatory wage and price controls in 1974 as the country struggled to deal with inflation, but in 1975 Trudeau imposed them on Canadians. Over the next four years, the Liberals exhausted their energy and their credibility – and Trudeau's charisma – as they struggled to deal with intractable economic problems. Trudeau concentrated on repatriating the country's constitution as a way of stirring the people of Canada, and in his speeches before the 1979 election he emphasized the need for Canadians to have their own constitution.

When the Conservatives under their new leader, Joe Clark, won that election, Trudeau showed that he had no liking for the role of Leader of the Opposition. In public he urged the Liberals to throw out the government, but in private he told friends that he did not want to be Prime Minister again. On 21 November 1979 Trudeau told his caucus, 'It's all over.' Then he had lunch with his estranged wife. Having bought a house in Montréal, Trudeau

Above: *By 1981, as Trudeau faced serious problems with the economy and worsening relations with the provinces, his previous light-hearted manner abandoned him in confrontational meetings with his ministers.*

Left: *Robert Stanfield, new leader of the Conservatives in 1972 after they won enough seats in Parliament to make Trudeau's a minority government.*

Above: *Trudeau (left) discusses the transfer of power to Prime Minister-designate Clark, who won in the 1979 election.*

Top right: *An unflattering view of Trudeau when he ran again in 1980.*

Left: *Trudeau campaigning in Chicoutimi, Québec, in 1979 for the forthcoming May election against Joe Clark.*

Right: *Re-elected Prime Minister in 1980, Trudeau turned his attention to the pressing problems of world tensions.*

Below: *Trudeau returns to office with his usual flair.*

SOMEBODY PAY THE BABYSITTER...

prepared to spend more time with his three sons. Although the voters had rejected him, many Canadians expressed their appreciation of Trudeau when he left politics. He had given Canada and Canadians a new image, a new mystique and a better feel for the modern world.

The Conservative government, defeated on a money bill in the House of Commons in December 1979, called an election for 18 February 1980. The Liberals pleaded with Trudeau to lead them again in an election. One cruel cartoon showed a patched, deflated Trudeau being pumped up to enter the lists. The Liberals swept Québec and Ontario, gained seats in Atlantic Canada and lost every riding west of Winnipeg.

At the victory celebrations, Trudeau, then 60 but still projecting a youthful image, spread his arms and

Right: *Among other forward-looking programmes, the Trudeau government launched Opportunities for Youth.*

said, 'Welcome to the Eighties.' The 1980s turned out to be worse than the 1970s. The Ottawa super-bureaucrats tightened their grip. The Liberal party had become a captive of Trudeau, and the Prime Minister, concentrating on giving Canada its own constitution, let the senior civil servants run the country. In his book *Up The Hill*, Cabinet member Donald Johnston outlined how the Liberal party withered at the grass roots as those in the Prime Minister's office and the Privy Council office acquired more and more power. While in Edmonton in 1981, Johnston received a phone call from the Deputy-Secretary of the Cabinet telling him that the government had decided to buy Petrofina, a foreign-

owned oil company, for $1.7 billion. At the time Johnston was President of the Treasury Board and responsible for government expenditure. He had not been consulted about the decision to buy Petrofina, nor had his Cabinet colleagues.

On 1 July 1982 Trudeau finally succeeded in giving Canadians their own constitution. It included a Charter of Rights and Freedoms that soon proved a bonanza to lawyers, as individuals and groups took to the courts to protect their interests. The Prime Minister turned his attention to international affairs and the gap between the rich and the poor in the world. In 1983-84 he tried to reduce world tensions by meeting with world leaders. This personal peace

Right: *On 10 March 1978 President Ronald Reagan (left) arrived in Ottawa for his first official visit with Trudeau.*

initiative achieved little, although Trudeau received the Albert Einstein Peace Prize for his efforts. On 29 February 1984, after a walk in the snow, Trudeau announced his decision to retire and left office on 30 June. The former Prime Minister moved into his art deco house in Montreal and joined a legal firm. He spoke at the PEN (Poets, Essayists and Novelists) Conference in New York in January 1986, urging the unruly assembly to be logical in their relations with the state and quoting Plato to support his point.

Even before Trudeau left office, his biographers expressed their bewilderment about him in the titles of their books – *Shrug* (Walter Stewart), *Paradox* (Anthony Westell), *The Northern Magus* (Richard Gwyn). Donald Johnston headed one of the chapters in his book *Up The Hill*, 'Who was Pierre Elliott Trudeau?' Only 20 years separate the resignation of Mackenzie King from the accession of Trudeau, and in the future, no doubt, academics will find in him as rich a source for research and speculation as they are finding in Mackenzie King.

Some of the Trudeau charisma still lingers. In September 1986 *Chatelaine* magazine named the 67-year-old former Prime Minister one of Canada's 10 sexiest men. Trudeau's political career reflected the turbulent times through which Canada passed in the 1970s and 1980s, and the way in which Trudeau approached problems shows a strong contrast to the style of his two successors as Prime Minister – Joe Clark and John Turner.

Top: *Trudeau during ceremonies in Ottawa when Queen Elizabeth II signed Canada's new Constitution Act.*

Above: *The Queen and Trudeau at dinner.*

TRUDEAU'S SUCCESSORS: JOE AND CHICK

The Rt Hon

CHARLES JOSEPH CLARK

4 June 1979 – 3 March 1980

The Rt Hon

JOHN NAPIER TURNER

30 June 1984 – 17 September 1984

When he becomes Prime Minister of Canada, he'll still be Joe to me.

MAYOR LUCILLE DOUGHERTY of High River, Alberta (1979)

Right: *Joe Clark was Canada's first western-born Prime Minister and, at forty, the youngest.*

On the morning after Charles Joseph Clark won the Conservative leadership race in February 1976, the headline in the *Toronto Star* read 'Joe Who?' The cartoonists and the media had a field day with Joe Clark. As one journalist put it, he was an 'altogether ordinary man' at a time when the public and the media wanted their politicians to be charismatic giants. How then did he become Prime Minister of Canada?

Born in High River, Alberta, in June 1939, Clark grew up in a small, tightly knit community where everyone knew everyone else. The Albertans there cherished the pioneer values of self-reliance and mutual aid. Clark's grandfather and father owned the community newspaper, *High River Times*. It reflected the world of the small town, which lay amid rolling land on which cattle grazed and wheat grew. To the west the Rockies fretted the sky, and just over 30 miles away lay Calgary, Canada's oil capital. In recent years High River has become a bedroom suburb of that city. At 16 Joe Clark won a Rotary Club public-speaking contest and an 'Adventure in Citizenship' trip to Ottawa, where he met politicians and watched the House of Commons descend into chaos during the Pipeline Debate over financing of a government scheme to bring western gas to the industrial east of Canada.

Clark left High River at 18 to attend the University of Alberta in 1957. He edited the student newspaper, organized demonstrations against the government, gained a reputation as a prankster and obtained a BA in political science. A tall, gangling individual, Clark fueled his frame with Coke and junk food, and gave his mind and his life over to politics. After graduation he drifted for a decade, attending law school in Halifax; obtaining an MA in political science; working at Harrod's in London; travelling in France, Spain and Italy; and assisting federal and provincial politicians in their campaigns. Elected MP for Yellowhead, Alberta, in 1972, Clark married Maureen McTeer in the following year. She retained her maiden name after marriage, much to the dismay of some older Conservatives.

Joe Clark came of age during the boom years that followed the Second World War. The West developed rapidly but retained its conservatism under surface optimism. Clark's win against 10 other contenders at the leadership convention in 1976 was not accidental. He represented the young and progressive end of the Conservative spectrum, committed to change, but gained his victory by a margin of only 65 votes over his closest rival, Claude Wagner of Québec. When the Progressive Conservatives came to power in a minority government in May 1979, Clark became the first western-born Prime Minister in Canada's history – and the youngest.

In public Clark appeared stiff and pompous. His unusual gait and naive curiosity attracted media attention. While Trudeau, with the assured arrogance of the academic, knew how to evade difficult questions, Clark appeared to be a perpetual student, unsure of the answers to questions that were posed to him. Clark spoke of Canada as a 'community of communities,' recalling the friendly world of his home town. Trudeau had a highly legalistic attitude towards the relationship between Canadians and the state. Clark, warm-hearted, courteous and generous in personal relations, provided a welcome relief in the corridors of power in Ottawa. But as a close friend put it, 'In this game you have to be a bit of a sonofabitch. Joe doesn't quite have it.'

Clark made two disastrous election promises – to move the Canadian embassy in Israel from Tel Aviv to Jerusalem and to dismantle Petro-Canada, the state oil company created by the Liberals. His government also promised a mortgage tax credit, but his attempts to tackle Canada's huge annual deficit undid his government. His Finance Minister John Crosbie, promising 'short-term pain for long-term gain' brought down his budget in December 1979 – and the government. When the NDP introduced a non-confidence motion, the Progressive Conservatives did not have enough members in the house to defeat it, and the Conservatives lost power.

As Leader of the Opposition, Clark slowed Trudeau's plans for giving Canada its own constitution to allow for more consultation with the provinces. Québec refused to sign the final document, and as the popularity of the Conservatives rose, some party members saw Clark as too progressive and a liability as a leader. Clark resigned his position and called for a leadership review in June 1983. He lost his position to Brian Mulroney. With characteristic generosity, Joe Clark helped to heal the wounds in the Progressive Conservative party. He fumbled as Prime Minister, but grew visibly in office and became the spokesman for a different vision of Canada, one based on a concern for community rather than on the machinations of rational bureaucrats. When the Conservatives took power in 1984, Clark became Secretary of State for External Affairs in the Mulroney government, and has acquitted himself well in that post.

Above: *During 1979 campaign, Conservative leader Joe Clark listens to a constituent in Ottawa, predicting that Trudeau's 'time is over.' In the election the following week, the Conservatives won and Clark became Prime Minister.*

Left: *The two prime ministers showed contrasting styles.*

Left: *Although his term of office as Prime Minister was brief, Joe Clark continued in service to the Conservative party and the government. He is shown here (left) as Secretary of State for External Affairs in the government of Prime Minister Brian Mulroney (right).*

Turner's so smooth, he's never made a mistake anybody can pin on him. He's the Liberal dream in motion.

BRIAN MULRONEY (1972)

Right: *As a Rhodes scholar John Turner studied law at Oxford and continued his education at the Sorbonne in Paris before returning to Canada and pursuing a legal and political career.*

On 10 September 1975 John Turner tendered his resignation as Minister of Finance to Prime Minister Trudeau. They chatted for an hour, and Trudeau asked Turner if he'd like to be a judge or a senator. Turner had hoped that the Prime Minister would offer him another portfolio, for he desperately wanted to stay in the government. He left Trudeau's office seething with rage.

John Napier Turner was born in Richmond, near London, England, in June 1929. His father, an English gunsmith with a mysterious past, had married a Canadian studying economics in London. Turner's father died when he was three, so his mother returned to her hometown of Rossland, British Columbia, then took a government job in Ottawa. Bright and beautiful, Phyllis Turner rose rapidly in the public service, while John attended Ashbury, a private school, and St Patrick's College, which was run by the Oblate Fathers. At the end of the war, Phyllis Turner married Frank Ross, a Scottish-born entrepreneur who subsequently became Lieutenant-Governor of British Columbia. The family settled in Vancouver, and John went to the University of British Columbia. He worked hard there, gaining many friends and the nickname 'Chick.' When he left to go to Oxford on a Rhodes scholarship, the student newspaper voted him the most popular student on campus. From Oxford, where he studied law, Turner moved on to the Sorbonne in Paris before returning to Canada to practise law in Montréal in 1953, earning about $100 a week.

A handsome, blue-eyed man, friendly to everyone, Turner gave a paper on legal aid at the Liberal conference at Kingston in 1960, and won a seat in the House of Commons two years later. Here he fell under the sway of the old Liberals, and served a long apprenticeship before entering the Cabinet and becoming Minister of Consumer and Corporate Affairs in 1967. Turner learned the many things that a politician had to do to gain and retain power – small favours, remembering names, observing the rules of the House of Commons, being polite to lawyers and judges and cultivating Cabinet colleagues. Pierre Elliott Trudeau never bothered with such trifles and beat Turner at the 1968 Liberal leadership convention, replacing Pearson as Prime Minister. He made Turner his Minister of Justice, and as such he piloted a massive bill to amend the Criminal Code and the Official Languages Act through the House of Commons. As Minister of Justice during the 1970 October Crisis, when FLQ members kidnapped the Minister of Labour and the British Trade Commissioner, Turner later claimed that the War Measures Act was 'too blunt an instrument' for handling disorder, and tried to bring in a milder Public Order Act.

Early in 1972 Trudeau assigned Turner to the Department of Finance, the graveyard of politicians. In the following year, Turner presented a splendid budget, borrowing ideas from the Conservatives and the NDP. He cut income taxes, raised old age pensions, and abolished taxes on children's clothes, candy and soda pop. Turner also wanted to cut the corporate tax rate, but found little support for the idea among his Cabinet colleagues. He favoured voluntary wage and price controls to curb inflation. However, the strain of trying to be an advocate of free enterprise in a government bent on intervening in all aspects of the economy proved too much for Turner, and he resigned in the fall of 1975. A cartoon in the *Ottawa Citizen* at the time showed Turner as General MacArthur above the slogan 'I shall return.'

After working with a corporate law firm on Bay Street in Toronto, Turner entered the Liberal leadership race in 1984. He promised to cut the deficit and to create jobs by restoring national confidence. After winning the leadership, Turner became Prime Minister in June, dissolved the House of Commons in July and ended up two months later as Leader of the Opposition with his party reduced to a rump of 40 members. At first, three members of the Liberal opposition, known as the 'rat pack,' nipped at the heels of Mulroney's new government. Gradually Turner gained control of the party and began rebuilding it from the grass roots. He also improved his speaking style. A thoroughly likeable and decent man who describes himself as 'a tactile politician,' John Napier Turner may yet become Prime Minister of Canada again as the Conservatives

struggle with tough economic times. The difficulties of Prime Minister Brian Mulroney, whose government came to power in a landslide victory in 1984, reveal many of the dilemmas of the man who controls most of the political power in Canada. Like his predecessors, he has found that great power brings great problems.

Above: As Minister of Justice during Trudeau's premiership, Turner piloted through the House of Commons a bill amending the Criminal Code and the Official Languages Act.

THE BOY FROM BAIE-COMEAU

The Rt Hon

MARTIN BRIAN MULRONEY

17 September 1984 –

. . . A large part of the Government's problems can be found at the top, in the persona of the Prime Minister. The negatives associated with his personality, his style and his credibility have overshadowed the policy accomplishments.

HUGH WINDSOR, 'PM Looks to Ways to Boost Sagging Popularity,' *Globe and Mail* (2 September 1986)

On 21 March 1974 a union official drove a bulldozer into the electrical generators at a construction camp on the James Bay hydro project in northern Québec. His actions cost the people of Québec $35 million, delayed work for several months and catapulted Brian Mulroney into the public eye. The official's action triggered a royal commission enquiry into the construction industry in Québec, headed by Robert Cliche. Mulroney served as one of the two other commissioners, and described its work as 'an unforgettable challenge: to clean up a vital sector of the economy that was corrupt from top to bottom.'

In his account of the commission, Mulroney describes himself as 'a Conservative lawyer, son of a unionized electrician from Baie-Comeau.' The present Prime Minister, like Joe Clark, came from a small community. He wrote of finding in Baie-Comeau 'a sense of regional solidarity, a spirit of mutual aid.' This 'instinct for co-operation has always enabled us to understand one another, to back each other up.'

His early life in the isolated paper-mill town on the north shore of the St Lawrence shaped Brian Mulroney's style. Baie-Comeau had been built by Robert McCormick, who wanted a secure supply of newsprint for his *Chicago Tribune*. Benedict Mulroney, Brian's father, helped build the paper mill and settled in Baie-Comeau to work on it in 1938. His son, born there in March 1939, grew up bilingual. Of Irish descent, the Mulroneys had friends among Anglophones and Francophones. Brian did well at school, but claims that he was 'one tough kid.' He also excelled in public speaking. During one contest, a man told his father: *'Ce gosse-là, il va faire un Chris' de bon évêque'* – ('That kid will

Far lower left: *Brian Mulroney campaigning with his wife Mila, who, he claimed, 'civilized me.'*

Left: *Mulroney at the Francophone Summit February 1986, when 41 French-speaking nations met at Versailles outside Paris.*

Below: *His role as a member of the Cliche Commission made Brian Mulroney a media star.*

make a hell of a good bishop.') The rough directness of this man's language reflects the nature of Baie-Comeau and the hopes that its residents had for their children.

In this instant community carved from the wilderness, the bosses held the power and the workers did what they were told in the single industry town. If you did not want to work at the mill, there were no other jobs. For an intelligent youth like Brian Mulroney, education offered an escape route. His father recognized this fact, and worked extra hours to provide the money for his children's education.

Brian Mulroney left Baie-Comeau in 1953 to attend St Thomas High School in Chatham, the New Brunswick town from which Prime Minister Bennett and Lord Beaverbrook started their ascent to power. Then Mulroney went to Saint Francis Xavier University in Antigonish, Nova Scotia. The university had been the centre of a Catholic social action movement in the 1930s. Much has been made of Mulroney's time in the home of the Antigonish movement. Father Moses Coady, its charismatic leader, stressed that intelligent people should serve their fellow men and women and not concentrate on personal advancement. His concerns have left no visible marks on Mulroney's personal or political style. Small in stature and deep of voice, Mulroney immersed himself in debating, drama and politics at the university, turning Tory in 1956. He supported John Diefenbaker at the Progressive Conservative leadership convention, and made much of his friendship with him at the university. In his senior year, Mulroney won the student elections and became Progressive Conservative Prime Minister in the Combined Atlantic Universities Parliament. Graduating with a BA in Political Science in 1960,

Mulroney attended Dalhousie law School in Halifax before deciding to return to Québec. He arrived at Laval University's Law School as the Quiet Revolution, organized by Québec's Liberals, swept Québec. Its goal was to achieve reforms in the economy, politics and education and to reassert the French culture. Canadians began asking, 'What does Québec want?' With some of his fellow students, Mulroney decided to provide the answer. In 1961 they organized a conference called *'Le Canada, expérience ratée or réussie?'* ('The Canadian Experiment, Success or Failure?')

During his days as a student Mulroney lived in residences in Chatham and Antigonish. During the summers he drove trucks and did other jobs at Baie-Comeau to pay his way through university. In the summer of 1962 he went to Ottawa as a special assistant to Minister of Agriculture Alvin Hamilton. Back at law school he decided to go into politics, but first he had to secure a steady income, so he planned to set up a law office in Baie-Comeau.

A friend told Mulroney of an opening as a *stagiaire*, or apprentice lawyer, with a large and prestigious Montreal law firm. Ben Mulroney urged his son to take this opportunity rather than returning to Baie-Comeau. Brian Mulroney often speaks of his father, of his devotion to his family and the sacrifices that he made for his children. Ben Mulroney's death in February 1965 deeply affected the young lawyer, who took responsibility for supporting the family he left behind. At the law firm, Mulroney worked hard. He also played hard, gaining a reputation as a brash and flashy man about town who loved fine clothes. He began dating an 18-year-old engineering student,

Mila Pivnicki, the daughter of a Yugoslavian psychiatrist, and married her in 1973. 'She civilized me,' Mulroney says.

At the law firm he established a reputation as a highly effective labour negotiator and mediator. He settled a strike at the Canadian British Aluminium plant at Baie-Comeau, helped to bring labour peace to the docks of Québec and defused tensions at *La Presse*, the Québec newspaper. Mulroney represented management on the Cliche Commission in 1974, which completed its task in a year and ushered in a new era in labour relations in Québec. The commission's revelations of corruption in the construction business, however, paved the way for the downfall of Robert Bourassa's Liberals, who lost power to René Lévesque and the Parti Québécois in 1976.

In that year Brian Mulroney stood at a crossroads. He could stay with the law firm, enter politics or accept the position of vice-president with the Iron Ore Company of Canada. The Cliche Commission had made Mulroney a media star, and the Progressive Conservatives were in poor shape in Québec. In the 1972 federal election they won two seats in the province, adding one more in 1974.

John Diefenbaker, beset by what he called 'termites' in the party, finally yielded his leadership to Robert Stanfield in 1967. This quiet man fixed his image – and sealed his political fate – by appearing on television eating a banana. No match for the charismatic, bilingual Trudeau, Stanfield stepped down gracefully from the Progressive Conservative leadership in 1975, and Mulroney decided to make a run for the position. Newspapers described him as

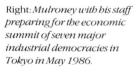

Right: *Mulroney with his staff preparing for the economic summit of seven major industrial democracies in Tokyo in May 1986.*

'dynamic, bilingual and seductive' with the 'carved in granite, made in heaven look that political publicists love to sell in public.' The Edmonton *Journal* compared his eyes with those of Paul Newman, his hair to Robert Redford's, his voice to Lorne Greene's and his chin to Gibraltar.

Despite all these qualities, Mulroney lost the leadership race to the uncharismatic Joe Clark, so he went to work for the Iron Ore Company of Canada, becoming president in 1977. In his intensive, energetic way, Mulroney moved restlessly around the company's properties in Labrador-Ungava, settling a strike; addressing company functions; honouring employees involved in volunteer work; and visiting mines, pellet plants and union halls. The prosperous days of iron mining and steel making were ending by the time he took over the company, which had been formed in 1949 to ensure a steady supply of iron ore for the steel mills of the United States. By 1983 all the mills in that country were running at just over half their capacity. Many used cheaper, richer iron ore from Brazil, and Canadian ore had to compete with this.

Schefferville, an instant town in the heart of Labrador-Ungava, had been the first centre of iron-ore mining. Mulroney presided over the closing down of the community, although he had managed to make a profit for the company while serving as its

Top: *In Toronto in 1985 Mulroney heads a fund-raising campaign.*

Above: *Mulroney celebrates Christmas with members of his Cabinet.*

president. An article in the September 1982 issue of *Canadian Business* called Mulroney 'the Tories' turnaround artist' and asked whether this 'closet Tory candidate' could 'run the country like he runs the Iron Ore Company.' The writer concluded, 'The country should be so lucky.'

In January 1983 two thirds of the delegates at the Progressive Conservative meeting in Winnipeg voted *not* to have a leadership review. Joe Clark decided to have one anyway, and Mulroney decided to enter the lists again. He spoke of 'One Canada' and claimed that the Progressive Conservative party remained on the Opposition benches 'for one reason alone – its failure to win seats in the French-speaking areas of the nation.' Mulroney believed that he could bring French Canada into the 'fullness and magnificence of Canadian life.' As he grasped for power, Canadians began to have a new image of themselves. The recession of the early 1980s jolted them into a realization that business, risk taking and entrepreneurship were needed in a highly competitive world. The radicals of the 1970s had become bureaucrats and academics, more concerned with their careers than with the plight of the poor and the disadvantaged. The country seemed to be stagnating while the Liberal government relied increasingly on reports, studies, commissions, experts, committees and polls for guidance. Both main parties saw the salvation of the economy in the private sector as the annual deficit shot past $30 billion.

Mulroney, the working man's son from remote Baie-Comeau, had shown what hard work, dedication, intelligence and initiative could do for one individual. He attracted outsiders to his leadership campaign and had an answer for every problem – 'We'll negotiate.' His approach sounded more and more reasonable as Trudeau increasingly used

Above: *The Prime Minister, with his Finance Minister, Michael Wilson (right), prepares the 1986 budget.*

Right: *Mulroney at First Minister's Conference in Halifax, November 1985.*

Left: *After the Tokyo Summit Mulroney visited mainland China and Korea. He is seen here with Deng Xiaoping in Beijing 10 May 1986.*

Below: *Canada's Prime Minister is given a gala welcome outside the Great Hall of Peace in Beijing.*

Above: *Prime Minister Robert Mugabe of Zimbabwe (left) with Mulroney at the Commonwealth mini-summit in London in August 1986.*

unseasoned timber. Mulroney appointed Stephen Lewis, former head of the Ontario NDP, as Canada's Ambassador to the United Nations. This move disappointed the party faithful, but reassured other Canadians of Mulroney's nonpartisan approach to international affairs.

Sir John A Macdonald had 13 members in his original Cabinet and Lester Pearson had 23 in 1963. Brian Mulroney appointed 39 new ministers, and the Cabinet soon became a sounding board rather than a decision-making body. Mulroney surrounded himself with cronies from his university days, and relied upon them and his daily scan of the media for direction. In the House of Commons he rose too quickly to questions posed by the Opposition, and the tough little kid from Baie-Comeau emerged from underneath the svelte exterior of the corporation executive. Mulroney appointed Erik Nielsen, the Yukon MP, Deputy Prime Minister. Nielsen presided over a number of task forces that examined every aspect of the government's operations, and earned the name 'Velcro Lips' because of his unwillingness to provide information or answer questions.

Some of the new ministers showed bad judgement in their portfolios, and the media delighted in detailing the errors of their ways. Solicitor-General Elmer MacKay talked to Premier Hatfield of New Brunswick about his trial for possession of marijuana. Minister of Defence Robert Coates admitted that he had visited a sleazy night club in Germany after a media story, and then resigned. Environment Minister Suzanne Blais-Grenier disturbed interest groups by making cuts in her department. She upset taxpayers even more when the media provided details of her expenses on a tour of Europe. She too resigned, as did Fisheries Minister John Fraser when cans of rancid tuna that his officials were supposed to have inspected went on the market.

Other ministers rose to the challenge of governing Canada. Joe Clark kept Canada's external relationships on a steady course. Minister of Finance Michael Wilson provided a $500,000 lifetime capital gains exemption to stimulate entrepreneurship, taxed the rich and promised to reform the entire tax system. Perrin Beattie humanized the Department of National Revenue, while Energy Minister Pat Carney began to dismantle the Liberal's National Energy Policy and made peace with the premiers of the western oil-producing provinces. Communications Minister Marcel Masse, initially seen as an enemy by the Anglophone cultural elite, emerged as a strong defender of Canada's culture.

The new government declared that the country was open for business, renaming the Foreign Investment Review Agency 'Investment Canada.' Mulroney initiated free-trade talks with the United States as feelings of protectionism rose there. When the Americans slapped a tariff on shakes and shingles from British Columbia, Canada retaliated with a duty on American books. The Canadian dollar fell, and began to hover above 70 cents American.

confrontation to solve his problems. Mulroney drew on the network of friends he had made at university to secure the leadership position. On 11 June 1983 Brian Mulroney beat Joe Clark on the fourth ballot by 259 votes. Elmer MacKay gave up his seat in central Nova Scotia, and on 29 August Brian Mulroney succeeded in winning 11,000 more votes than his Liberal opponent.

When John Turner called an election for 4 September 1984, Mulroney decided to run in Manicouagan, the riding in which Baie-Comeau lay. As he put it, 'I have to go home.' He defeated his opponent by 21,000 votes, and the Tories took 211 seats in a landslide victory. The Conservatives captured 50 percent of the popular vote. The Liberals, with 28 percent of the vote, secured only 40 seats and the NDP, with 19 percent, obtained 30 seats.

Once in power, Canada's eighteenth Prime Minister faced the usual problems of governing a country with a party that had not held office for any length of time for almost 20 years. He also had made promises to individuals and interest groups, but developed few policies. For his Cabinet he could choose between some old wood and some new,

The business community recognized the need to cut the deficit, as did many other Canadians, but every time the Prime Minister moved to reduce government expenditures, his ministers faced a barrage of criticism from interest groups that benefited from federal grants and programmes. A proposal to de-index old age pensions in May 1985 released the fury of seniors and the government backed down.

In an era during which most people were more concerned with personalities than politics, the achievements of the Conservative government remained unheralded as ministers became involved in scandals. Between June 1984 and June 1986 the economy grew by 9 percent, creating 679,000 new jobs. Yet the government had an image problem, traceable to the Prime Minister. The experiences of the new government reaffirmed what is very apparent throughout Canadian history. Because of the peculiar nature of the Canadian government, the fate of the party lies with the way in which voters view the Prime Minister. Many Canadians liked their local Tory MPs, but viewed Mulroney as paying too much attention to an inner circle of cronies. While preaching the gospel of restraint, the Prime Minister poured millions into his riding and showed expensive tastes when he travelled abroad. Mulroney had promised to clean things up after Canadians protested about the way in which Trudeau handed out perquisites and posts when he left office, but he seemed to favour his friends at the pork barrel as much as his predecessor did. Given to hyperbole and boasting, the Prime Minister had gained a reputation for talking a great deal and saying very little of substance. He did not want to tell Canadians the harsh facts of life, and many people became disillusioned over the gap between Mulroney's promise and his performance.

Above: *The prime ministers of Great Britain and Canada, Mrs Margaret Thatcher (left) and Brian Mulroney (right), meet at the British Prime Minister's official residence, 10 Downing Street, in London in August 1986.*

Right: *Mulroney with the Aga Khan (left) and his wife (right) in Vancouver August 1985.*

Left: *On a visit to Washington, DC, 18-19 March 1986, Prime Minister Mulroney (at podium) had numerous discussions with President Reagan (seated, left).*

Right: *The Royal Visit of Prince Charles and Princess Diana to Expo '86.*

Below: *Japan's Prime Minister, Yasuhiro Nakasone (left), is welcomed on his visit to Canada in January 1986.*

In June 1986 a Gallop poll showed that 40 percent of the decided voters would favour the Liberals and only 32 percent the Conservatives. That gave the governing party only 5 percent more of the decided vote than the NDP, and its popularity dropped sharply in Québec. Mulroney shuffled his Cabinet, dropping Yukon Erik. A national pollster, however, noted in July 1986 that 'the cabinet shuffle does not address the fundamental election issue – the relationship of the Canadian Prime Minister.' Mulroney, like every other Prime Minister, is the living embodiment of Canada. Canadians project their hopes, dreams, aspirations – and fears – on to him. One columnist accused Mulroney of 'equivocation, overstatement, glibness,' but it may be that Canadians are seeing in the head of their government the qualities they cannot abide in themselves.

In August and September the Prime Minister and Cabinet members toured Québec and Atlantic Canada to make closer contact with Canadians. The West, which had boomed a few years ago, began to feel the bite of a recession as oil, wheat and other commodities fell in price. Premiers in the western provinces began to complain of feeling 'alienated' from Canada.

Canada is certainly a difficult country to run. In recent years, however, Canadians have come to appreciate what holds them together rather than what separates them. Nothing is certain in politics. In 1988 it looks as if Canadian voters will be asked to choose between political parties headed by two remarkably similar men. Both Brian Mulroney and John Turner started with very little, became corporate lawyers and rose to positions of prominence in Canada by hard work. Both have a desire to reinterpret old political philosophies and to make them relevant to a country adrift in the currents of change.

How each presents himself and his policies will be the deciding factor in the next election. Whoever becomes Canada's next Prime Minister will be able to look back down the corridors of time and learn to appreciate how others have handled the role. And in doing so, he might learn better how to create unity out of the diversity of Canada and Canadians.

Top: *Brian Mulroney with his wife and children.*

Left: *Holding his one-year-old son Nicolas in a crowd at St George de Beauce, Québec, August 1986.*

Right: *Mulroney greeting celebrants on Canada Day 1986.*

INDEX

Picture Credits

Bettmann Newsphotos: pages 129(top), 132, 133(top left and center), 138, 139(top), 140, 141.
Bison Picture Library: pages 4-5, 57(top), 76, 110(bottom), 154(top).
Canada Department of National Health and Welfare/Public Archives of Canada: page 129(bottom left).
Canadian Consulate General: pages 8, 9(both), 10(bottom), 11, 12, 13, 35(right), 37(bottom), 51, 91(bottom), 93, 94, 98(top), 99(bottom), 103(bottom), 106-07, 109(bottom), 111(bottom), 113, 119(both), 121(right), 124, 125, 127(top), 130(bottom), 131(both), 134(both), 135(both), 136, 137, 144.
Canadian Embassy: page 123.
Canadian Pacific Corporate Archives: pages 18-19, 22(both), 23(all three), 26-27(bottom), 31(both).
City of Toronto, Archives: page 61(top).
Confederation Life Collection: pages 2-3, 6-7, 14-15, 20(both), 21, 24(bottom), 32(both).
Glenbow-Alberta Institute: pages 27(center), 44-45, 71(center and bottom), 72(bottom), 73(top).
Government of Quebec: page 126(top right).

Ted Grant/National Film Board of Canada/Public Archives of Canada: page 129(bottom right).
House of Commons, Canada: page 29.
Information Canada: page 10(top).
National Film Board: pages 1, 96(top), 101.
Newark Public Library Picture Collection: page 27(top).
Photo Centre Library-SSC/Karsh: page 143.
Prime Ministers Office, Canada: pages 139(bottom), 145(both), 146, 147(both), 148(both), 149(both), 150, 151(both), 152, 153(both), 154(bottom), 155.
Provincial Archives of Alberta, E Brown Collection: page 44(inset).
The Public Archives of Canada: pages 17, 24(top), 25(both), 26(top), 30, 33(both), 34(both), 35(left), 37(top), 39(top), 40, 41(both), 42-43, 43, 46-47(both), 48(both), 52-53, 54(all three), 55, 56-57, 58(both), 59(all three), 60, 61(bottom), 63, 64(both), 65(both), 67, 68, 69(all three), 70(top), 71(top), 72(top), 75, 77(all three), 78, 79(both), 80(top), 82-83, 83(center), 86(inset), 86-87, 88-89, 89(inset), 90(bottom), 91(top), 95, 96(bottom), 97, 99(top), 105, 114, 115(both), 116(top), 118(top left and bottom), 126(bottom).

Rt Hon J G Diefenbaker Centre: pages 102, 103(top), 104(both), 106(bottom), 108, 109(top left).
Saskatchewan Archives Board: pages 45(inset), 70(bottom), 71(top), 73(bottom), 107(bottom).
Toronto Star Syndicate: pages 109(right), 110(top), 111(top), 118(top right), 120(top left), 127(bottom), 128, 133(bottom), 139(center).
United Nations: pages 90(top), 116(center and bottom).
Edd Uluschak: page 133(top right).
WW: pages 80(bottom), 81(both), 83(top and bottom), 84(inset), 84-85, 98(bottom), 117, 120(top right), 120-21, 126(top left), 130(top).

Acknowledgments

The author and the publisher would like to thank the following people who helped in the preparation of this book: Susan Garratt, who edited it; Sue Rose, who designed it; Jean Chiaramonte Martin, who did the picture research; Florence Norton, who wrote the captions and prepared the index.